THE FIRST SCHLESWIG HOLSTEIN 1848-50

Nick Svendsen

1848 was a turbulent but momentous time in Europe. Within this context, the Duchies of Schleswig and Holstein were caught between the rising nationalism and desire for unification of the Prussian/German nation states and the traditional alliances with the Danish Kingdom. The Schleswig Holsteiners decided that allegiance with the German Federation, including possessing their own constitution, was the best way forward. They rebelled against the Danish and looked to the Prussians with their greater military prowess for help. In Denmark, as in other European countries, the call for a democratic constitution caused social disturbance, triggered initially by the February riots in Paris. The Danish monarchy, in crisis, both constitutionally and in terms of monarchical succession continued to lay claim on their southernmost duchies and sent their armed forces to destroy the Schleswig-Holstein insurgents.

The author describes the battles and battlefields upon which this crisis was played out: from the first major action at Bov (9 April, 1848) to the last major battles of the war, at Isted (25 July 1850) and Missunde (12 September 1850), from the geomorphic landscape influencing battlefield strategy down to the description of a farmhouse where Prussian officers jumped out of windows to save themselves from the Danish. The reader is led through this war and shown the changing battlefields during this momentous period of European history.

This book is profusely illustrated with black and white images including battle maps, and also includes four superb colour uniform plates. Full orders of battle, for all armies, are also provided.

Nick Svendsen was born in Copenhagen, Denmark, in 1948. He graduated from Copenhagen University in 1975 as a geologist and joined the oil industry in the same year. He has since worked as an exploration geologist. The work made him visit many places outside Europe such as North Africa, Middle East, America and the Far East. He has always been interested in all aspects of history, and this book is the result of this interest. The interest in the Schleswig wars comes from the many visits to the Armoury museum in Copenhagen which is close to where he lived in the childhood. He has published a number of papers on geological subjects. This book is his first publication on a historical subject. He is married and lives in Denmark.

THE FIRST SCHLESWIG-HOLSTEIN WAR 1848-50

Nick Svendsen

Helion & Company Ltd

Helion & Company Limited
26 Willow Road
Solihull
West Midlands
B91 1UE
England
Tel. 0121 705 3393
Fax 0121 711 4075
Email: info@helion.co.uk
Website: http://www.helion.co.uk

Published by Helion & Company 2008
This paperback reprint 2009

Designed and typeset by Helion & Company Limited, Solihull, West Midlands
Cover designed by Bookcraft Limited, Stroud, Gloucestershire
Printed by Lightning Source Ltd, Milton Keynes, Buckinghamshire

Text © Nick Svendsen 2007
Maps © Nick Svendsen

Cover image: 'Episode of the Battle at Dybbøl on 5 June 1848' by Niels Simonsen (painted c1850), showing Danish artillery (rear cover), and Danish infantry advancing in skirmish order (courtesy of the Museum of National History, Frederiksborg Castle).

ISBN 978-1-906033-44-6

British Library Cataloguing-in-Publication Data.
A catalogue record for this book is available from the British Library.

All rights reserved. No part of this publication may be reproduced, stored in a retrieval system, or transmitted, in any form, or by any means, electronic, mechanical, photocopying, recording or otherwise, without the express written consent of Helion & Company Limited.

For details of other military history titles published by Helion & Company Limited contact the above address, or visit our website: http://www.helion.co.uk.

We always welcome receiving book proposals from prospective authors.

Contents

List of Illustrations vii
List of Plates ix
List of Tables x
List of Maps xi
Acknowledgements xiii
Foreword xiv
Introduction xv

Chapters

1 The Road to War 17
2 Landscapes and wars 27
    The maps used by the armies 29
    The organisation of the armies 31
    The weapons of the armies 36
    The Navies during the First Schleswig War 40
3 1848 46
    The Battle at Bov 46
    The Battle at the town of Schleswig 53
    Sundeved 28th and 29th May 1848 66
    Sundeved June 5th 1848 73
    The period until the armistice 74
    The naval operations in 1848 77
    The armistice period from August 1848 to April 1849 78
4 1849 80
    Sundeved 1849 82
    The navy operations and the affair at Eckernförde 83
    North Jutland until Fredericia 88
    Fredericia 92
    The Armistice 103
5 1850 107
    The Battle at Isted 107
    The naval operations in 1850 114
    The period until the end of the war 116
    The period after the war 121

Appendices

A Statistical tables 123
B Orders of Battle 132

C	Colour uniform plates	142
D	Infantry arms	149
E	Guns	151
F	The war expenses	152

Bibliography 154

List of Illustrations

Fig. 1.1	Christian August, Duke of Augustenborg	20
Fig. 1.2	Friedrich Emil August, Prince of Nör	21
Fig. 1.3	Friedrich Wilhelm IV of Prussia	22
Fig. 1.4a	King Frederik VII of Denmark	23
Fig. 1.4b	Prime Minister, Count A. W. Moltke	23
Fig. 1.5	The Provisional Government in Schleswig Holstein	24
Fig. 1.6	Prince Nör in the Rendsburg coup	25
Fig. 2.1	Map of the Sundeved area and the island of Als	30
Fig. 2.2	Company column formation used at Bov 9th of April 1848	32
Fig. 2.3	Stretcher bearers	34
Fig. 2.4	Dressing station	35
Fig. 2.5	Transport of wounded	36
Fig. 2.6	Infantry weapons	37
Fig. 2.7	Cavalry weapons	38
Fig. 2.8	84 pound light howitzer of 1834	38
Fig. 2.9	6 pound solid ball gun of 1834	39
Fig. 2.10	An espignol with a calibre of 15 mm	40
Fig. 2.11.1	The Royal Danish Navy – type of ships	41
Fig. 2.11.2	The Royal Danish Navy - type of ships	42
Fig. 2.12	A rowing gunbarge of the dinghy type in action	42
Fig. 2.13	*Brandtaucher*	44
Fig. 3.1	Anton Frederik Tscherning	48
Fig. 3.2	Hans Christoph Frederik Hedemann	49
Fig. 3.3	Verner Hans Frederik Abrahamson Læssøe	50
Fig. 3.4	The battle at Bov April 1848 3rd Chasseur Battalion	51
Fig. 3.5	The battle at Bov April 1848 2nd Chasseur Battalion	52
Fig. 3.6	During the last phase of the battle around Flensburg	53
Fig. 3.7	Friederich Heinrich Ernst Wrangel	54
Fig. 3.8	The guns at Bustrup	57
Fig. 3.9	Captain Würtzen's attack at Hysby, 1848	62
Fig. 3.10	The 2nd Chasseur battalion at Oversø	63
Fig. 3.11	Christian Frederik Hansen	64
Fig. 3.12	Sundeved on 28th and 29th of May 1848	71

Fig. 3.13	Cristoph von Krogh	75
Fig. 3.14	Eduard von Bonin	76
Fig. 4.1	Karl Ludwig Ernst von Prittwitz	82
Fig. 4.2	The Eckernförde affair	87
Fig. 4.3	Frederik Rubeck Henrik Bülow	88
Fig. 4.4	Olaf Rye	91
Fig. 4.5	The fighting at the Trelle redoubt on 6th of July 1849	101
Fig. 4.6	The death of General Rye at the Trelle redoubt	102
Fig. 4.7	Carl Wilhelm von Willisen	106
Fig. 5.1	General Frederik Adolf Schleppegrell	109
Fig. 5.2	The battle at the village of Isted 1850	111
Fig. 5.3	Christian de Meza	113
Fig. 5.4	A view of the battle at Friederichstadt 4th of October 1850	118
Fig. 5.5	Danish troops at the Dannevirke rampart	116
Fig. A1	Chasseurs firing	149
Fig. A2	Muzzle loading infantry weapons	150
Fig. B1	A smoothbore gun with associated equipment	151

List of Plates

1. Danish Troops I 145
2. Danish Troops II 146
3. Schleswig-Holstein and German Troops I 147
4. Schleswig-Holstein and German Troops II 148

List of Tables

1	The size of the army	123
2	The artillery	123
3	The Danish and Schleswig Holstein Navies	124
4	The gunboat flotillas	126
5	Localities and alternative names	127
6	Casualties during the war	129
7	The cost of the war 1848–50	130

List of Maps

1	Denmark and Schleswig Holstein	16
2	Europe and the German Federation in 1848–1850	18
3	Geological map of Jutland	28
4	The battle at Bov 9th of April 1848	47
5a	The battle at the town of Schleswig April 1848 (1): Skirmishes 15th - 23rd April 1848	55
5b	The battle at the town of Schleswig April 1848 (2): The German advance 23rd April 1848	56
6a	The battle at the town of Schleswig April 1848 (3): 10:00–12:00 hours	58
6b	The battle at the town of Schleswig April 1848 (4): 12:00–13:30 hours	59
7	The battle at the town of Schleswig April 1848 (5): after 13:30 hours	61
8	Sundeved 28th May 1848 - situation before the battle	65
9a	Sundeved 28th May 1848 (1): 12:00–15:00 hours	69
9b	Sundeved 28th May 1848 (2): 15:00–20:00 hours	70
10	Eckernförde 5th April 1849	84
11	General Rye's retreat in 1849	90
12	Fredericia	93
13	Fredericia from 7th May to 6th July 1849	95
14	Fredericia 6th July 1849	100
15	Isted 24th July 1850	108
16	Isted 25th July 1850 until 9:00 a.m.	110
17	Isted 25th July 1850 until 12:00 noon	115
18	Schleswig 1850 - battles and skirmishing	117
19	Friedrichstadt 27th September 1850	119

Acknowledgements

I would like to thank my wife and my family for their patience during family holidays when they were forced to visit old battlefields and listen to explanations about where the various units clashed. I would especially also like to thank Gavrielle Groves Gidney who reviewed an early version of the manuscript and for her valuable proposed revisions to the manuscript. Former Director of Orlogsmuseet (the Danish navy museum) in Copenhagen, Ole Lisberg Jensen, reviewed the manuscript and commented especially on the description of the navies and the naval actions. His valuable comments have been incorporated. My wife reviewed the Danish translation and her valuable comments are incorporated.

Foreword

When I first became interested in the history of the war in Schleswig Holstein 1848–1850, I was only a child. My father had bought a booklet which had been published in 1948 to celebrate the centennial of the war. It mostly contained pictures which made it easy for a small boy to digest. This first exposure was the starting point for my interest in history.

Many years later the same subject caught my attention again but this time I continued the study using the military library in Copenhagen. There are a large number of books on the wars in Schleswig which are mostly in Danish and German with only a few summarised accounts in English.

My studies were eventually put down in manuscript form in Danish but I soon realised that the book could be brought to a wider audience by being translated into English.

Introduction

Between the years 1848 to 1850 the peoples of the Duchy Schleswig Holstein and Denmark were at war (Map 1). This conflict is called the First Schleswig War. The second war was fought in 1864 but this time between Denmark and Prussia/Austria.

These wars were the result of many things such as changing power structure in Europe, growing nationalism, the beginnings of democracy, the conflict between the Duke of Augustenborg and the Danish King as well as changing economic structures between the Duchy and the Kingdom of Denmark.

The whole process became even more complicated because the larger European nations of the time got involved in the conflict. Denmark was in a transition between absolute monarchy and democracy. The new democracy had politicians who were not skilled in state diplomacy and foreign policy with the eventual catastrophic outcome of the second war in 1864.

The conflict in 1848 to 50 was a civil war, which separated friends and families. Christian of Glüksborg, who later became King Christian IX of Denmark, served in the Danish army while he had most of his family supporting the Schleswig Holstein side. This family schism has never been healed. General Krogh, commander of the Danish army in 1849 and 1850 had a brother who fought with the Schleswig Holstein Army. The Danish general Rye, one of the Danish heroes from the war, was considering not participating in the war as he was sure to fight old friends.

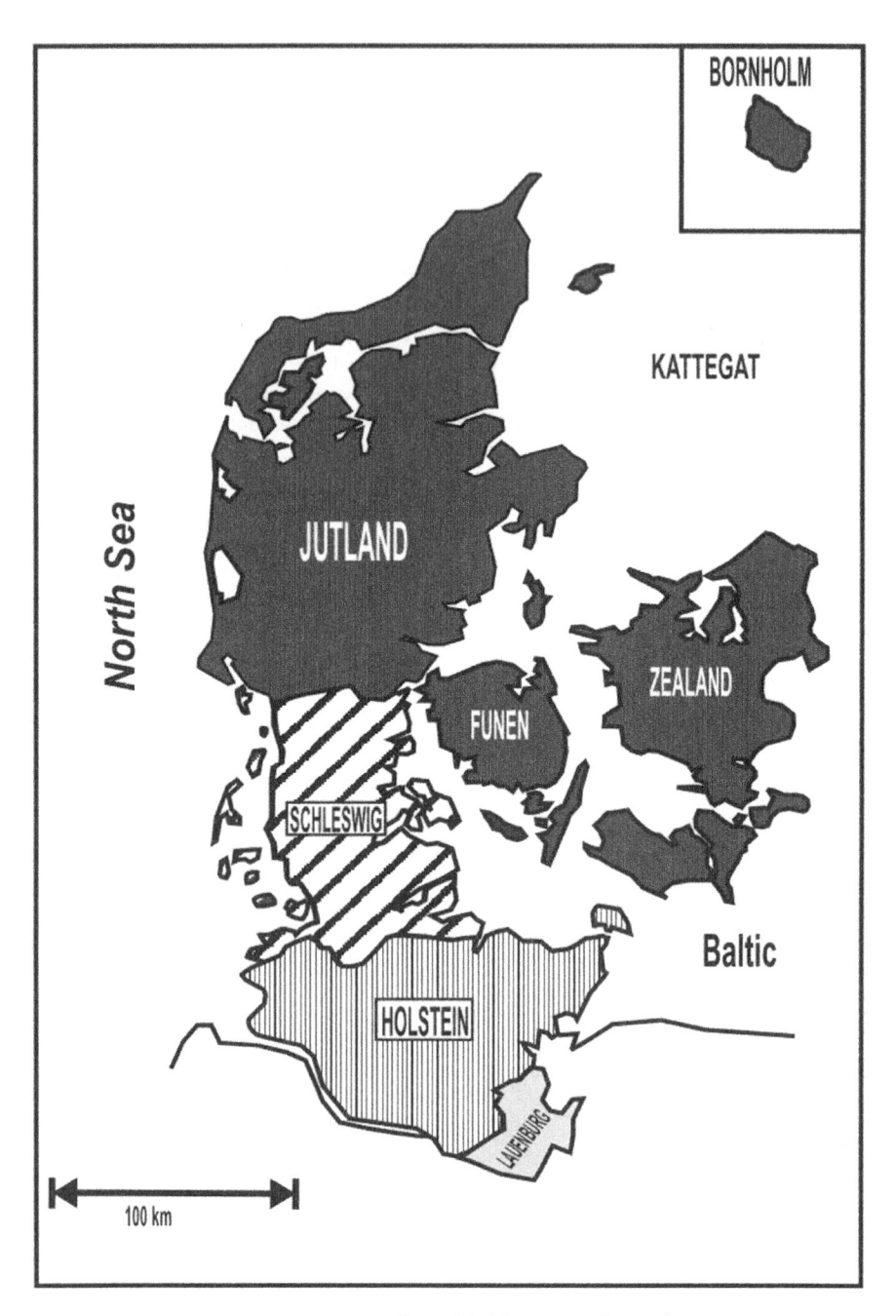

Map 1 Denmark and Schleswig Holstein

Chapter 1

The Road to War

The Duchy of Schleswig is situated at the base of the Jutland peninsula (map 1). The old border between the Kingdom of Denmark and this Duchy was situated at a stream called the King's River (*Konge Åen*) which is north of the current border. The southern border of the Duchy is the river Eider. The Duchy of Holstein is the land between the Eider and Elb Rivers.

The Kingdom of Denmark is the remaining part of Jutland north of the King's River, Funen, all the islands around Funen, Zealand, and before 1658, also Scania, Halland and Bleking in southern Sweden (ceded to Sweden after several wars).

The Duchy of Schleswig was the old borderland between the Danish and the German speaking peoples. Charles the Great created his Carolingian Empire by conquest of most of Europe in the years before 800. His empire ran from Italy in the south to the Eider River in the north. However, the conquest of Saxony which Holstein was part of, took 30 years and was not completed before 804. During this period the Saxons made several bloody attempts to get free of the Carolingian hegemony but their efforts were in vain.

The Danish King Godfred saw Charles the Great as a significant threat to his power and therefore supported the Saxons' resistance. In order to defend his realm he expanded the rampart called the Dannevirke. The first part was built around year 700 AD.

This defence system is situated at the southern border of the Duchy of Schleswig some 25 km north of the river Eider (map 2). The manning of the Dannevirke required an army. As the Danish king could not be present at all times in the borderland he needed a proxy and that was the Duke of Schleswig. So the later King Valdemar the Victorious made his son, Abel, Duke of Schleswig in 1232. King Valdemar had several sons who were appointed dukes of the other borderlands as was the custom at that time. It is this arrangement which is the seed for the later conflicts between the Duke of Schleswig and the King of Denmark.

Abel was often in conflict with the King and in alliance with the Schleswig Holstein dukes. When Abel's last descendent died in 1375 the wealthy and powerful counts of Holstein took over the Duchy of Schleswig as a vassal to the Danish King.

Holstein belonged to the German empire and the Counts were therefore also vassals of the German emperor. Eventually the last of the descendants of the Holstein counts died in 1459 and the Danish king Christian I, (crowned 1448), had the right to take the Duchy of Schleswig back as a reverting realm. However, he also wanted to take control of the rich Duchy of Holstein and therefore had himself elected by the Assemblies of the Estate of the realms for both Duchies as Duke of Schleswig and Count of Holstein.

The election took place in 1460 in the town of Ribe in the northern part of Schleswig. He signed a document where he promised to keep the peace and to keep the Duchies together for all time ("*ewige tosamende ungedelt*").

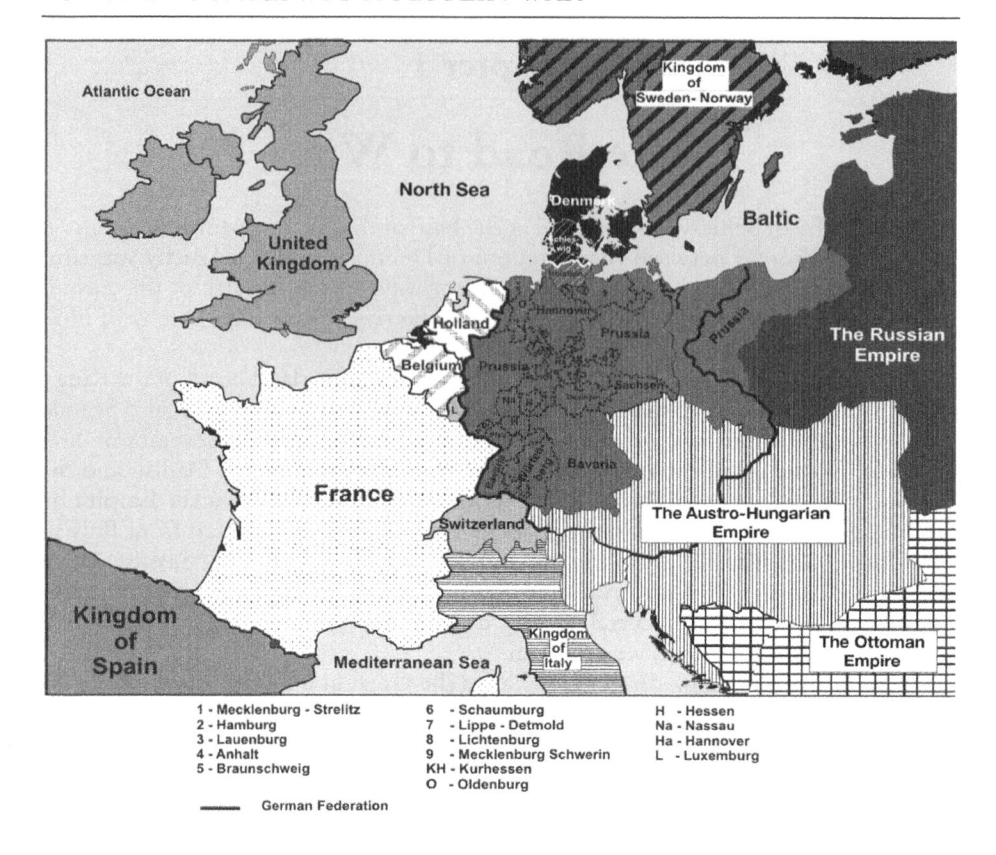

Map 2 Europe and the German Federation 1848–1850

In the subsequent years Schleswig Holstein was nevertheless split into a royal part and into a part which was given to the King's brother who became Duke of Gottorp. This led to further dispute where the Duke of Gottorp often supported enemies of Denmark.

During the Great Northern War in 1709 to 1720 between Denmark and Sweden, the Duke supported the Swedes who were defeated, and the King of Denmark, Frederik IV took over the sovereignty of the Duchies. The King demanded an oath of loyalty from his sovereignties and released them from their loyalty to the Duke of Gottorp. All the nobility of Schleswig Holstein were called to the castle of Gottorp and on 4th September 1721 they (including the Dukes of Augustenborg and Glücksburg) all signed a declaration of loyalty and acknowledgement of the Law of the King. Frederik adhered to precedent and therefore ruled Denmark as King, and the Duchies as Duke. The realms had common finances and defence but were otherwise were administered separately.

Although Danish was spoken in the southern portion of Schleswig in the old times, the German language became more and more common further north. In 1848 the border between the German and the Danish speaking populations was approximately where it is today (the current border between Denmark and Germany).

After the fall of the Emperor Napoleon in 1814, the allied European nations took power and at the peace of 30th May 1814 it was decided to settle all the European disputes at a Congress in Vienna that same year. All the dominant countries of Europe were represented as well as the Danish King Frederik VI. The German Confederation which was abolished by Napoleon was reinstated and Holstein became a member (map 3). However, Frederik VI resisted Schleswig's Confederation membership as he stated that it had always been Danish.

Norway, who was in union with Denmark, was ceded from Denmark the same year and given to Sweden. The Danish king was compensated in Germany with the Duchy of Lauenburg (map 1). He was then king of Denmark and Duke of Schleswig Holstein and Lauenburg.

The Napoleonic wars from 1796 to 1814 were for Germany a battle of independence from the domination of France. It was also the time when nationalism came to Europe, in particular to Germany. After the English attack on Copenhagen in 1807, Denmark joined France and declared war on Britain. The German speaking part of Schleswig Holstein did not sympathise with this alliance.

The English blockade of Europe during the Napoleonic wars had a negative effect on the economy of both Denmark and Germany, due to the lack of overseas trade. Furthermore the last battles of the war took place in Schleswig Holstein, where Danish and Schleswig Holstein troops fought together (for the last time) against the allied troops (Swedish, German and Russian) led by the Swedish king.

In 1813 Holstein was occupied by mostly Swedish and Prussian armies after the end of the hostilities. The population had to supply these armies during the wintertime, which was never forgotten and remembered as the 'Cossack winter'.

After the reorganisation of Europe where Norway was ceded from Denmark, the Duchies constituted of only about 40% of the population in the Danish King's realm and the German influence was increased.

The Schleswig Holstein nobility therefore tried to increase its influence in 1822 by having Schleswig incorporated into the German Confederation. The Danish King strongly resisted this. There was no support for the incorporation from the Parliament of the Confederation in Frankfurt so for the next eight years nothing happened.

The absolute Danish monarchy from 1814 to 1848 was in its last phase before democracy was introduced. After the July revolution in France in 1830, liberal movements arose all over Europe including Denmark and Schleswig-Holstein. The demand from the liberals was for a democratic constitution. In order to suppress the liberals, the Danish King had a number of them arrested and jailed.

According to the Vienna Congress of 1814 Holstein was entitled to a new constitution and the parliament of the German Confederation in Frankfurt demanded that the Danish Government prepare one. The Danish King had to do something and therefore a commission was initiated and asked to work on a draft constitution.

In 1834 the work of the commission was finished. The result was four Assemblies of the Estates of the Realm *(Stænderforsamlinger)*, one for the islands of Zealand, Funen and Bornholm with representatives also from Iceland and the

Faerø Islands (assembly place Roskilde near Copenhagen), one for Jutland (assembly place in the town of Viborg in Central Jutland), one for Schleswig (assembly place in the town of Schleswig) and one for Holstein (assembly place in the town of Itzehoe). The members of the assemblies were partly appointed by the King and partly elected by the population.

The right to vote was only available to men above the age of 30 who had land or income worth a value between 1000 and 4000 *Rigsbankdaler* subject to where they were living (the highest income was in Copenhagen). Hence only a minor part of the population was able to vote.

The election for the assemblies took place in 1834 and later that same year, they had their first meeting. It was in these Assemblies of the Estates of the Realm that the German and Danish interests clashed. The German and Danish Liberal movements had in essence the same goal, a new and free constitution. However, the German liberals were allied with the Pan-Germanic movement whereas the Danish Liberals had an affinity to the other Scandinavian countries.

The Pan-Germanic movement was nationalistic. Germany was at that time divided into many small states (map 2) and the movement argued for a united Germany. The liberals of Schleswig Holstein sympathised and demanded that Schleswig, like Holstein and Lauenburg, should join the German Confederation and that the three Duchies should have a common constitution.

It was recollected that King Christian I of Denmark in 1460 had issued the letter in the town of Ribe, which declared that Schleswig and Holstein should be

Figure 1.1 **Christian August, Duke of Augustenborg (1798–1869)** became duke in 1814 after his father. He was the elder brother to the Prince of Nör and In contrast to his brother, who was very impulsive, he was a cool and calculating politician.

Figure 1.2 **Friedrich Emil August, Prince of Schleswig Holstein Sønderborg Augustenborg, also called the Prince of Nör (1800–1865).** The Prince of Nör was officer and in 1848 Major General in the Danish Army. During the first year of the war he commanded the Schleswig Holstein Army, but in September of the same year, when General Bonin took over the command he resigned from the army. In 1851 he was expelled from Denmark and the Duchies. Thereafter he stayed in Germany and also for a while in London. There was no use for him after the war in 1864 and in 1865 he died on a trip to Egypt.

together and undivided. On the other hand the Danish population wanted Denmark's southern border to be at the river Eider.

King Christian VIII, who became king in 1839 when Frederik VI died, tried to find common ground between these two trains of thought in an attempt to keep his realm together.

An issue was what language should be used in the two Assemblies of the Realm for the Duchies. So far the language had been German but the Danish-speaking members asked for permission to speak Danish. This was rejected but a petition was sent to the King. He eventually declared that if a member was not able to speak German he was allowed to speak Danish.

The Danish Christian VIII's son, the later Frederik VII had no children and therefore no heir. The law of the King (the old constitution) did not apply to Holstein but it was disputed that it was applicable to the Duchy of Schleswig. Christian August, the Duke of Augustenborg in South Jutland was a close relative to the royal family and therefore raised the claim that he should inherit the Duchy of Schleswig when King Frederik VII died. This dispute, the issue whether the Duchies should join Germany, the language and the issue of a new constitution was the conflict between the two population groups.

22   FIRST SCHLESWIG HOLSTEIN WAR

Figure 1.3 **Friedrich Wilhelm IV of Prussia (1795–1861).** Friedrich Wilhelm IV became king in 1840 until his death, although his brother Wilhelm I was constituted as king in 1854 due to Friedrich Wilhelm's poor health in his last years. On 18th March 1848 Friedrich Wilhelm had proclaimed a free constitution and when the citizens of Berlin gathered around the castle to applaud him they were shouting "Away with the military". The troops had just arrived in the city and were ordered to remove the mob. The soldiers opened fire and killed a number of people, which ignited the rebellion (photo from Wikipedia 2007)

Between 1830 and 1848 these differences expanded until the rebellion in 1848.

The Duke of Augustenborg (figure 1.1) was part of a sub-branch of the royal family and, as mentioned, closely related through later marriages. Queen Caroline Mathilde Queen of Denmark married to the Danish King Christian VII had a daughter with her lover Struense. This daughter Louise Augusta (1771–1843) was half sister to King Frederik VI and married Friedrich Christian of Augustenborg (1765–1814). In this marriage there were three children: Christian August (1798–1869), Friedrich Prince of Nör (1800–1865), and Caroline Amalie (1796–1881). The latter was married to King Christian VIII of Denmark.

Augustenborg is situated on the Island of Als and was a large estate.

Christian August, a cool and calculating politician, became Duke in 1814 inheriting the title from his father. His brother, the Prince of Nör (figure 1.2) in contrast was very impulsive.

The Prince of Nör was very popular and therefore elected to the Assembly of the Realm where he was a member of the conservatives. In 1842 he was appointed as Governor and commanding General in the Duchies by the King. Two years later he resigned as Governor, as a protest against the open letter from the King

Figure 1.4a **King Frederik VII of Denmark (1807–1863)**

concerning the royal order of succession which was not in either his or his brother's favour.

Christian August was sometimes in opposition to his brother, especially in 1842 when Nör was appointed Governor, an appointment which Christian wanted for himself as part of his political plans. Christian had in 1837 raised the question about the royal succession in an anonymous publication. He believed that he and his family would be the closest to inherit the Duchies after Fredrick VII.

The Augustenborg family had been considered for the Danish crown but Christian August's political activity did not make him popular in Denmark and

Figure 1.4b Prime minister (*konsejlspresident*), **Count A.W. Moltke,** of the government of 22nd March 1848.

with the King. Christian VIII tried to solve the matter of the royal succession by the issue of an open letter which said that the declaration of loyalty of 1721 made any earlier claims null and void and the law of the King was therefore effective in Schleswig but that it could be disputed in Holstein.

The letter made the Augustenborg family and many others in Schleswig Holstein furious. The King and his government were strongly criticised in the Duchies and in Germany. This created a considerable animosity against Denmark all over Germany.

1848 was the year of revolution in Europe. It commenced in France with the rebellion against King Louis Phillipe of France, who had to leave Paris on 24th February 1848, a provisional government being formed. It was there that the ideas of democracy emerged and it stemmed from the middle classes, which demanded power. However, shortly after the first revolution the workers of Paris rebelled against the new provisional government. This was the event, which also ignited insurrection in Schleswig, Holstein and Denmark. In Germany civil unrest erupted, and in March of the same year there were revolutions all over Germany – e.g., 1st March revolution in Baden, 3rd March demonstrations in Cologne and on 5th March a rebellion in Heidelberg.

In Vienna on 19th March the Duke Metternich was dismissed and the Emperor of Austria was forced to construct a democratic constitution. King Ludwig of Bavaria abdicated on 19th March and his son Maximillian took over.

In Berlin there was a demonstration in front of the royal palace. King Friedrich Wilhelm IV of Prussia (Figure 1.3) ordered the military to intervene. Overnight there were fighting in the streets of Berlin leaving many dead and wounded.

Figure 1.5 The Provisional Government in Schleswig Holstein, "the Statholders", was formed on 24th March 1848 in the town hall of Kiel. The first action of the "Statholders" was to declare the rebellion. The members are from the left in the first row: Bremer, W.H.Beseler, Th. Olshausen, and Count F. Reventlow. In the second row are M.T. Schmidt and Friedrich Prince of Nör.

Figure 1.6 On 24th March 1848 the Prince of Nör took a platoon of soldiers and some citizen from Kiel to Rendsburg where the commandant was taken by surprise. The garrison was assembled and the Prince read the proclamation from the Provisional Government. It stated that the Danish King was no longer free and a Provisional Government had been formed for Schleswig Holstein. The Prince was wearing a Danish general's uniform. After he had made his proclamation he requested those who would not join him to step forward. Many of the officers then stepped forward and the Prince declared "I do not mean you". The officers then were given time to reconsider. Some escaped and the rest were later released on the condition that they did not join the Danish army. The rest of the garrison joined the Prince.

The next day the King had to apologise and in order keep face he blamed the military for the violence. The officers of the army were furious and the King had lost prestige. Conveniently, Christian August the Duke of Augustenborg had just arrived in Berlin on 23rd March in order to ask for help from the Prussian King to solve the conflict in Schleswig Holstein. It was just what Friedrich Wilhelm IV needed. He ordered the army to leave Berlin and it marched towards Schleswig Holstein. The King also submitted a letter to the Duke in which he declared his wishes to support the Schleswig Holstein cause. He furthermore asked the German states which supplied troops to the 10th Confederate Army Corps to send troops to Holstein. The King had revived the old trick of finding an external enemy to divert attention from the internal crisis.

Christian VIII died on 20th January 1848 and Frederik VII became king of Denmark (figure 1.4). In his first meeting with the cabinet a new constitution was discussed. The cabinet agreed to recommend a common constitution for the Kingdom and the Duchies.

On 8th March there was a general meeting of the populace in Copenhagen in a theatre called Casino to discuss "Denmark to the River Eider".

In Schleswig the populace demanded a democratic constitution for the Duchies and in a meeting of the Assembly of the Estate of the Realm it was decided to send a delegation to Copenhagen.

In a new meeting in Casino on 20th March the liberals of Copenhagen demanded a new government and a democratic constitution for the Kingdom and Schleswig. It was decided to send a deputation to Frederik VII the next day to deliver the demands. So the next day a big crowd assembled at the Copenhagen town hall square and at noon it moved towards the castle of Christiansborg.

The King had dismissed his Cabinet when the demonstration of the citizenry of Copenhagen reached the royal palace; they met the dismissed ministers on the way out of the palace. The King could therefore tell the delegation that their demands had been met. A new government was formed with representatives from both conservative and liberals with Count A. W. Moltke as Prime Minister.

When the Schleswig Holstein delegation arrived in Copenhagen they negotiated with the new government without any results.

With the rumours of what happened in Copenhagen, the Schleswig Holstein leaders assembled in Kiel on 23rd March. They agreed to form a provisional government for Schleswig Holstein called the 'Statholders'. On 24th March the Prince of Nör travelled to Rendsburg with a platoon of soldiers and citizens of Kiel. With a coup he succeeded to convince most of the garrison of Rendsburg to join the provisional government.

The rebellion in Schleswig Holstein was now a fact and on 29th March 1848 the Danish army marched into the Duchy of Schleswig.

Chapter 2
Landscapes and wars

The landscape of Jutland can be divided into three different geomorphologic provinces: the flat heath landscape to the west, the hilly boulder clay landscape to the east and north, and the marsh landscape to the south-west (map 3).

The interplay between these three landscape types have for centuries had a significant effect on transport and communication as well as the outcome of any military conflict.

The boulder clay landscape, situated on the eastern side of Jutland, is very hilly and cut by several so-called tunnel valleys (glacially eroded valleys) which can be fairly long, are mostly east-west oriented and up to 2,000 m wide. The boulder clay was deposited by the glaciers during the last Ice Age.

Most of the valleys host a stream and lakes. In many cases the sea transgressed the eastern end creating a fjord (e.g. Schlie or Horsens fjords). Those valleys have always, and still do, exhibit significant obstacles to north-south transport.

To the west is the widespread heath landscape. It is mostly flat and sandy and was deposited by rivers of melting water running to the west from the edge of the glacier. Today it is also cut by rivers such as Ribe å, Trenen and the Eider. While these rivers have been useful for barge transport they are also obstacles for land transport. Before intensive agricultural use there were also many wetlands in the form of bogs. The heath landscape was generated during the last Ice Age by the many melt water rivers which ran from the glaciers and towards the west out into the North sea. The rivers deposited mostly sand and gravel.

Consequently the main transport road has always been and is still situated at the watershed between the two landscapes. This is called the Army or Oxen Road. It runs from the town of Viborg in the north, to south of Rendsburg. This old road was previously used for driving cattle to the markets in north Germany, an important export commodity since the Middle Ages. It takes six days to travel by horse from Viborg to Rendsburg. The old defence system, the Dannevirke, consisting of several ramparts, is situated on the southern part of the peninsula and runs perpendicular to the Army Road and thus controls it. Even today the modern highway is placed close to the Army Road.

It was along this road that the Swedish army in the late part of the1600s invaded Denmark and it was here that most of the battles of the Schleswig wars took place.

Both landscape types continue south into Germany. The *Lüneburger Heide* is an extension of the heaths of western Jutland and Schleswig.

The last landscape type is the marsh. It is an extension of the heath landscape and is flat and swampy. When the sea transgressed the western part of Jutland after the glaciers of the Ice Age had melted away it reached further inland than the coast today. Slowly fine grained fertile sediments were deposited and gradually the coast moved west to the current position.

For a long time the people living here have been able to utilise this area for agriculture and cattle breeding by building protective dikes and digging canals to

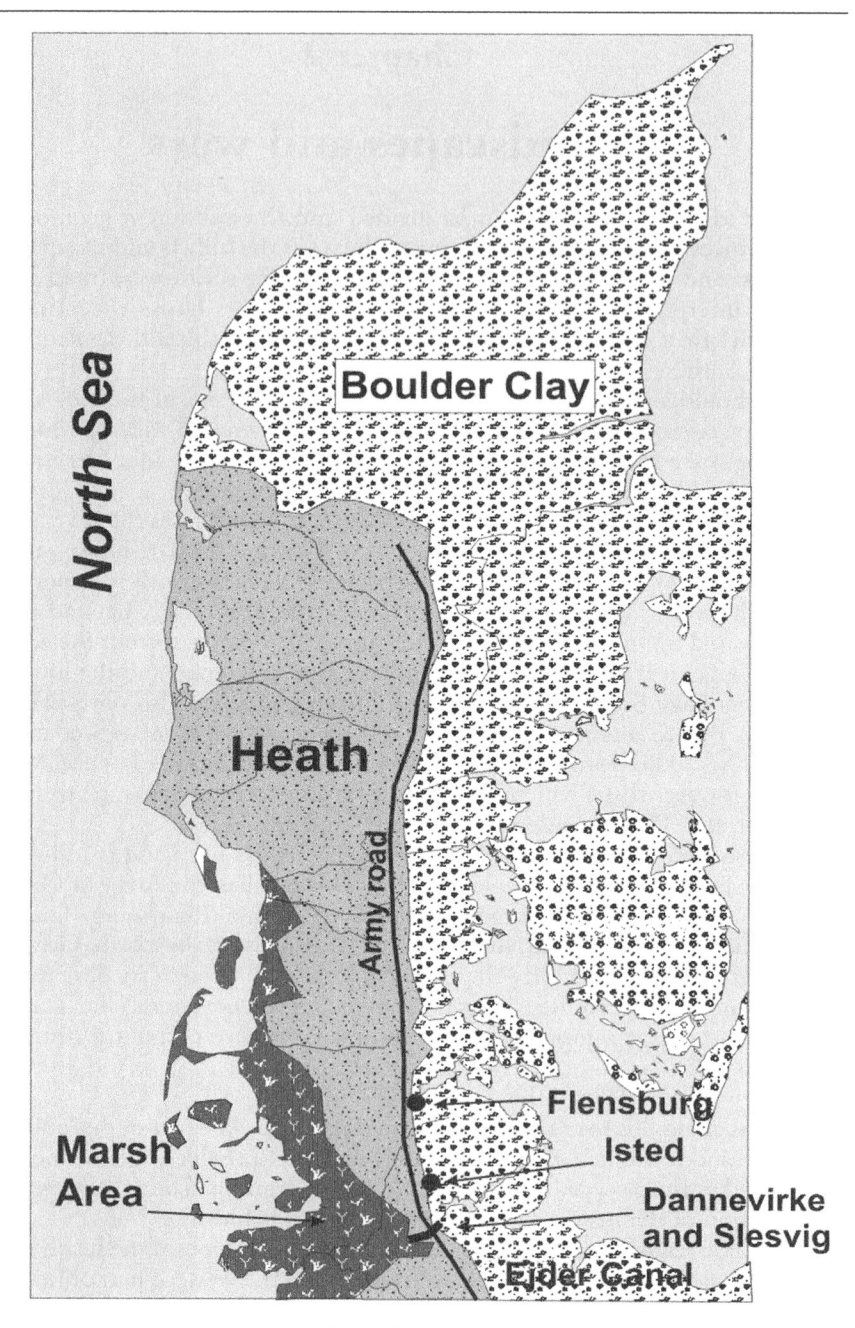

Map 3 Geological map of Jutland
A geological map of Jutland and Funen showing distribution of three major landscape types, the boulder clay, the heath and the marsh areas.
The Dannevirke rampart is situated where the heath area is a narrow strip between the fjord and the wetlands of the marsh.

drain the soil of water. In the past it was nearly impossible to take an army with its load of heavy weapons (cannons, etc) through this wet landscape apart from the winter months when it was frozen. These wetlands were therefore easy to defend. The fjords were difficult to cross especially if the opponent had a navy to defend them. The Dannevirke is therefore situated on the high ground between the fjord of Schlie in the east and the wetlands to the west where an enemy of Denmark was forced to pass through in case of an attack on Denmark.

In 1800 Denmark was a seafaring nation (as today) and had, despite the drawback of 1807, where the British navy captured most of the Danish navy, been able to build a new naval force. Prussia and the German states on the other hand had only a small navy in those years. Therefore, in theory, Denmark had the naval advantage along the coastlines and the impassable wetlands.

In the Duchy of Schleswig there are three places where the landscape offers good defence possibilities and they are all situated where the fjords meets the heath landscape and where rivers of the heath landscape make a natural barrier to the west. The three places are at Flensburg, Isted and the town of Schleswig (map 3).

At Isted for example there is a tunnel valley running east-west, with a lake called 'Langesø'. To the west is the river Trenen. Furthermore wetlands make passage difficult. These obstacles reduce the defence line from 13 km to 6 km.

A similar situation exists at the town of Schleswig. Here it is the fjord of Slien, which creates an eastern barrier and, to the west, it is Trenen. The Dannevirke is placed immediately south of Schleswig.

At Flensburg an attacking army is forced to go through the town of Flensburg due to the fjord of Flensburg and the river Trenen.

It was at these three places the initial and the last battles of the First Schleswig war in 1848 to 1850 took place and it was here that the Danish army tried to defend itself against the Prussian and Austrian armies in the Second Schleswig war in 1864.

The maps used by the armies

In order to orient in a landscape a geographical map is required over the place of the battlefield. The maps (figure 2.1), which were available in 1848, were somewhat different from those of today. The mapping of Denmark had commenced in the eighteenth century by the Danish Academy of Science. Those maps do not have contour lines nor coordinates but illustrate terrain differences by different hatching. The mapping was surveyed in the scale of 1:20,000 but printed in the scale of 1:120,000. The Danish Army had, however, in 1842 commenced a more modern mapping of Denmark where elevation differences were illustrated with contour lines like in modern maps. This work was far from finished at the onset of the war in 1848. The Army therefore used the old or some sketchy maps.

All these maps can be used for overall planning but for the detailed operations (e.g. artillery shooting) reconnaissance or local knowledge was still required.

The Schleswig Holstein Army presumably had the same maps available in the first part of the year but during the armistice period cartographers were sent out to work in the battlefield areas. In 1850 they had mapped the important areas including Schleswig and Isted. The maps are not more detailed than the Danish ones but they are on a smaller scale.

30 FIRST SCHLESWIG HOLSTEIN WAR

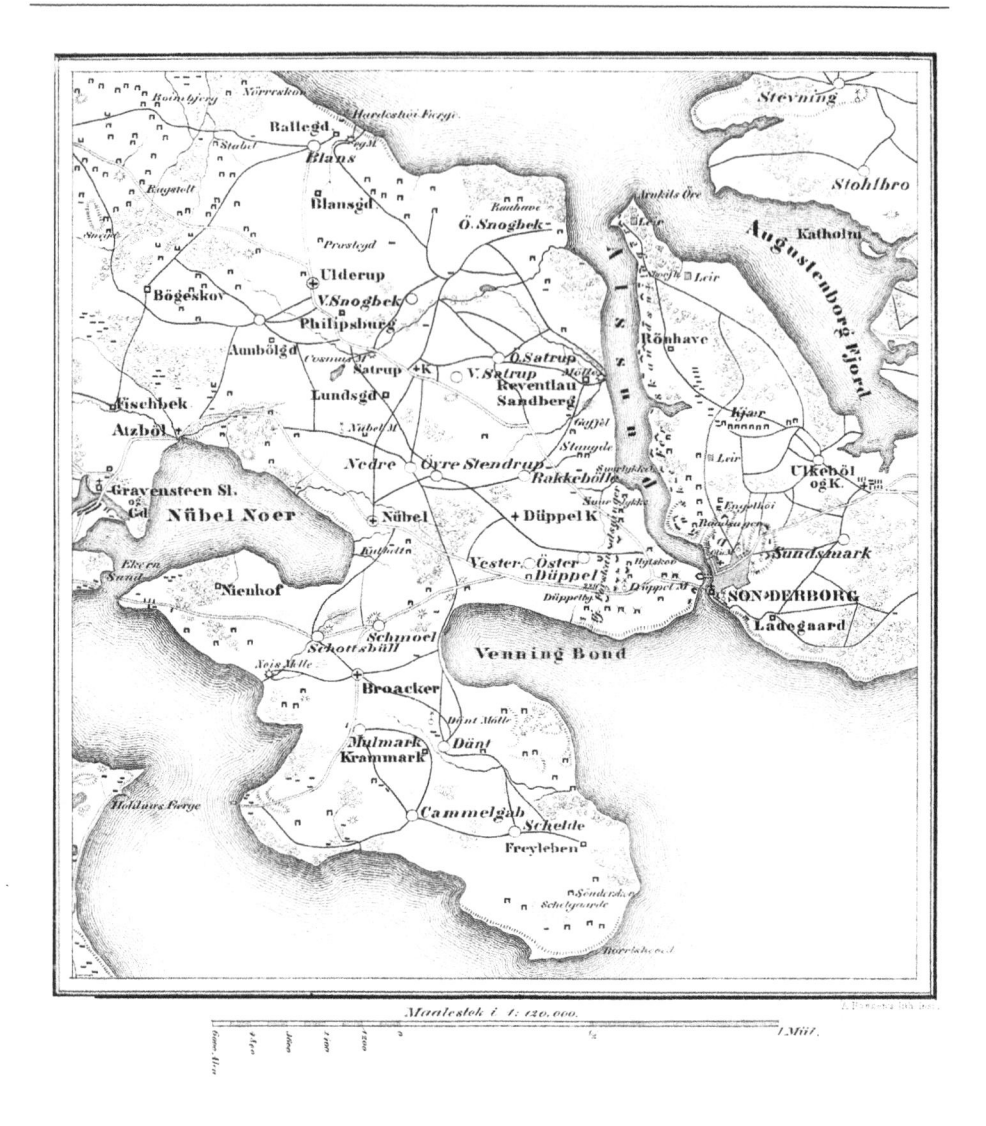

Figure 2.1 Map of the Sundeved area and the island of Als in northern Schleswig. The map is from 1852 and must represent what knowledge was available at the time. The first systematic mapping was conducted by the Danish Academy of Science and issued in 1825. The army had taken over the mapping of Denmark since 1825. Colonel Læssøe had been part of the mapping team in the years prior to the war. The map is useful for orientation and planning of larger military operations. It lacks coordinates which hampers detailed planning and artillery shooting.

The organisation of the armies

The armies of the past were heavy in infantry, i.e., they consisted mostly of foot soldiers. The mobile part of the army was the cavalry, which served as an offensive unit, as well as reconnaissance and dispatch riders. The artillery played an important role too. The armies also had engineering and medical corps. The transport service consisted of horse-drawn carriages confiscated from the local peasants. The army therefore moved by foot and horse. It was not until the war in 1864 that railway became a significant means of transport.

In addition to this the Danish army was highly dependent on sea transport between the bigger islands Zealand and Funen to the peninsula Jutland and for this purpose the navy was used.

The task of the engineering corps was to prepare defensive positions and generally remove any hindrances for the artillery as well as building or destroying bridges.

The operational unit of the army was the battalion, which in 1848 consisted of 800 men, in 1849 1,000 men and in 1850 1,100 men. The battalion was divided into four companies. The operational unit of the cavalry was the squadron of 180 men with horses. Four squadrons made a cavalry regiment. Three to four battalions with a squadron and an artillery battery constituted a brigade which was used for independent operations. In 1850 another unit was introduced: the division, which was used for the first time in the battle at Isted in 1850. The division consisted of three to four brigades. The Danish Army used in 1848 and 1849 the term 'Corps' for a unit which is comparable to a division. As 'Corps' in English military terminology covers a unit including several divisions it has been translated as Division although this term was not used before 1850.

The Danish army consisted of the Regular Army and the Reserve. This constituted the men in the age range from 22 to 30 years and only men of the peasantry. Men over 30 years but less than 45 years were in the reinforcement. This organisation was introduced in 1842 as part of an Army reorganisation but never fully implemented. At the beginning of the war the Regular Army and the Reserve consisted of 24,000 men; however 8,000 of these were from Schleswig Holstein. After the Schleswig Holstein battalions mutinied the Danish army had a strength of 16,000.

In order to strengthen the army but not destroy the farming work supporting the Danish economy only 22-year old recruits were enlisted. Volunteers from the cities not employed in farming were asked to enlist. Looking at the age distribution of the Danish population in 1848 the 22 year olds constituted some 24,000 men of which ca. 50% were related to farming. The new government did a lot to raise volunteers and organised these into voluntary corps, which later were merged into the existing battalions. There were also a number of volunteer officers from both Norway and Sweden.

As part of the new democratic constitution, compulsory service was introduced from September 1848 so that the army in 1849 had the strength of 41,000 men (table 1).

At the rebellion the 14th, 15th, 16th and 17th Battalions, the 4th and 5th Chasseur battalions, the 1st and 2nd Dragoon Regiments, the 2nd Artillery

32 FIRST SCHLESWIG HOLSTEIN WAR

regiment and some engineering units mutinied. These units made up the initial part of the Schleswig Holstein army. The Prince of Nör organized this army so that 14 through 17 Battalions were numbered I through IV and the Chasseur battalions were renumbered I and II. Three new battalions numbered V, VI and VII were formed from the reserve which was called in. The volunteers which came from Germany were formed in so-called free corps. They were however released early on in July 1848 due to their poor performance and lack of discipline.

The formation of the Battalion in battle

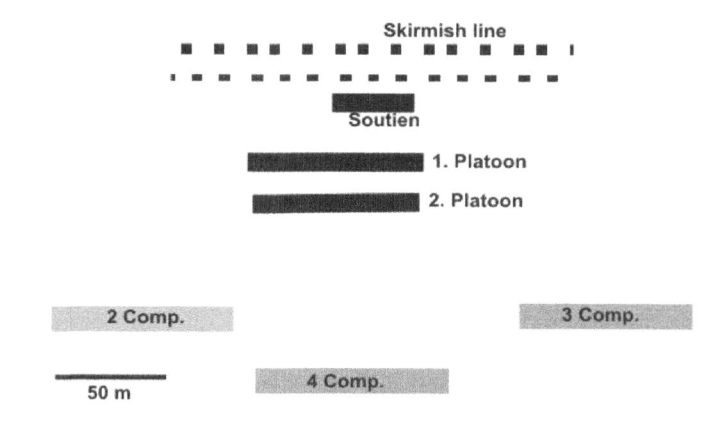

Skirmish line

Soutien

1. Platoon

2. Platoon

2 Comp.

3 Comp.

50 m

4 Comp.

Based on Vesterdal 1978

Figure 2.2 Illustration of the company column formation used at Bov 9th April 1848. The Danish infantry is moving forward with two skirmish lines - in the front the first platoon, and behind the second platoon. The three reserve companies are seen behind (in the front of the picture). The Schleswig Holstein units are present on the hill.

The training period for the newly conscripted in the Danish army was eight weeks which was used mostly for disciplinary training, learning commands, horn signals and battalion formations. The training in sharpshooting took only a short time whereas the handling of the guns was more thorough.

The Prussian Army was divided into the Regular Army and the Landwehr of first and second line. There was compulsory service of five years in the Regular Army of which three years was in active service. After five years they were transferred to the Landwehr where they remained until 39 years of age. The Landwehr was mostly used for local defence and it was therefore only battalions of the Regular Army that came to Denmark.

The infantry companies were formed in two platoons of three lines each. During attack a line of skirmishers was formed from the third line from each of the two platoons. The line was backed up by a small reserve called a *soutien*. The line of skirmishers was formed some 100 metres in front of the company. Each soldier stood about ten paces from the other while the *soutien* was formed in a close line behind as support e.g., during retreat. This formation was called 'company column' (figure 2.2) and was introduced in Denmark under the Army reorganisation in 1842 and in Prussia in 1847.

As a result of the development of small arms since the Napoleonic Wars there was a need for a more flexible and less massive infantry formation. It was the first time the 'company column' formation was tested and it worked well. The *chasseur* companies were divided into two sections of each two platoons, slightly different than the normal infantry companies. Each platoon had two lines and either could be used as skirmishers. As the muskets were muzzle-loading the riflemen supported each other in groups of two men: while one was shooting the other was loading.

The battalion had four companies that could form different battle positions where two or three of the companies worked as reserves for the others which went into battle organised in company column. The reserves were always formed in tight lines. The skirmishers moved towards the enemy (figure 2.2) and if they could not drive them away the reserve moved forward, opened fire and attacked with their bayonets.

The cavalry was mostly used for reconnaissance or pursuit of retreating enemies. The Danish cavalry Brigade was operating in Jutland as a mobile independent unit. However, it soon became apparent that without infantry support it was not strong enough for larger operations. For instance, after the battle at Bov (1848) and Isted (1850) the cavalry attempted to pursue the Schleswig Holstein army but could not stop them.

Infantry weapons with a long range made a cavalry attack very perilous. The cavalry had therefore lost its offensive power and mounted fighting on a large-scale as known from the Napoleonic wars happened only twice during the three years of war: at Århus in Central Jutland in 1849 and at Jagel south of the town of Schleswig in 1850.

At the onset of the war the Danish army had 800 officers, however not all were suited for a command in war. The Danish officers were trained by the Academy for Army officers. In order to increase the numbers, more command schools were opened. An organisation for Officers of the Reserve had been initiated also but did not work properly. Instead non commissioned officers were promoted.

Figure 2.3 After the battles the wounded were collected and brought back to the field hospital. Each company had a stretcher.

During the war some 520 officers were commissioned from the schools so that the army at the end of the war had 1,130 officers, which means that some 190 of them were killed or dismissed.

Generally speaking the Danish commanders performed well during the war although there were examples of misconduct.

Schleswig-Holstein officers were also in short supply at the onset of the war as not all of the officers of the mutineer units joined the Schleswig Holsteiners. To bolster ranks for the Schleswig-Holstein Army, Prussian officers were transferred. These were educated at the *Kriegs-Schule* in Berlin, which had teachers such as Clausewitz, the famous author of 'On War' (*Vom Kriege*). The school was one of the best in Europe and yearly field manoeuvres added to the training.

The Schleswig Holstein officers had the same education as those of the Danish army. At the end of 1848 the Schleswig Holstein Army had 305 officers of which half (149) were from the other German countries but mostly Prussia. At the end of the war the total number were 890 of which 506 were from other countries.

At the outbreak of the war, the Danish army was dressed in red jackets, blue trousers and shako (see colour plates). The chasseur battalions were dressed in green uniforms. During the war the uniform was changed to a dark blue coat, blue trousers and a blue field cap. But this change was not fully accomplished before 1850. The cavalry got blue uniforms whereas the coachmen and the medical corps kept the red jacket. The soldiers wore a knapsack with supplies for 24 hrs with a weight of ca. 10 kg.

The Schleswig Holstein army had initially modified Danish attire. However, their regular troops soon got Prussian uniforms (plate 2) whereas the chasseurs got

Figure 2.4 The military doctors and the orderlies had the so-called 'cantina knapsack', a first aid box. The dressing station was marked by a green flag with a white cross. It should be remembered that Red Cross did not exist before the Second Schleswig Holstein War in 1864.

a green jacket with black shako different from the Prussian. The cavalry had a blue uniform.

Conducting a large army requires communication and co-ordination of the various army units. Mounted dispatch riders delivered written or oral orders. The battalions and companies used horn signals. The battalion bugler knew 20 to 30 horn signals used to direct the soldiers to advance or retreat. Apart from these signals, bonfire and gunfire were used but not always with success.

An army requires constant supply in order to be able to function. In this regard all transport of munitions and food supplies were carried out by conscripted peasant horse carriers. By 1848 the Danish army organised its own transport units by the purchase of a large number of carriers, so that each battalion had eight or ten carriers available with supplies and munitions. A large number of donations of horses at the beginning of the war from the population ensured sufficient horses for the carriers. Actually there were more than needed.

The medical units were organised in the first days of the war. Three field hospitals were prepared and followed the Danish army to Jutland. Each hospital had three doctors and seven stretcher-bearers. Each company carried one stretcher (figure 2.3). Behind the lines larger hospitals were organised, which could receive the wounded after the first treatment in the field hospitals (figure 2.4). The wounded were transported in carriages requisitioned from local peasants (figure 2.5).

There is a battlefield statistic, which covers dead on the battlefield, dead in the hospitals within three weeks or wounded (see Appendix A). A wound could be

Figure 2.5 The army bought special ambulance carriages, however most transport of wounded to the field hospitals behind the front took place in carriages requisitioned from the local peasants. The comfort for the wounded was improved by placing straw in the carriage. The wounded were brought from the field hospitals to the larger hospitals behind the front.

serious, as the knowledge about antiseptic treatments was limited, with many soldiers dying of infections.

There is a story about the secretary of war A. F. Tscherning visiting one of the hospitals after the battle at Bov in 1848. He tumbled over a bucket with arms and legs, the result of various amputations. He then asked the doctor in charge if this was not too drastic and if fewer amputations would do. The doctor replied snappishly – 'Your Excellency we are at war'. There was not time for more mild treatment and amputation was the only solution. At the outbreak of the war there were not enough doctors so the army conscripted students and others with less or no education as orderlies. These people often had to treat the wounded without help from the doctors and not always with good results. In the battle at Bov the field hospitals quickly became crowded with wounded resulting in chaos. However during the winter the medical corps were reorganized and with time, they improved their performance..

The weapons of the armies

The infantry mostly carried muzzle loading smoothbore muskets (figure 2.6). However the chasseur battalions had muzzle loading pillar rifles. The smoothbore muskets had a firing range of 150 m whereas the rifles had a range of 450 m. Nevertheless the soldiers preferred the smoothbores because they were faster to load which was critical in pitched battle (Appendix A). On average 17% of the Danish

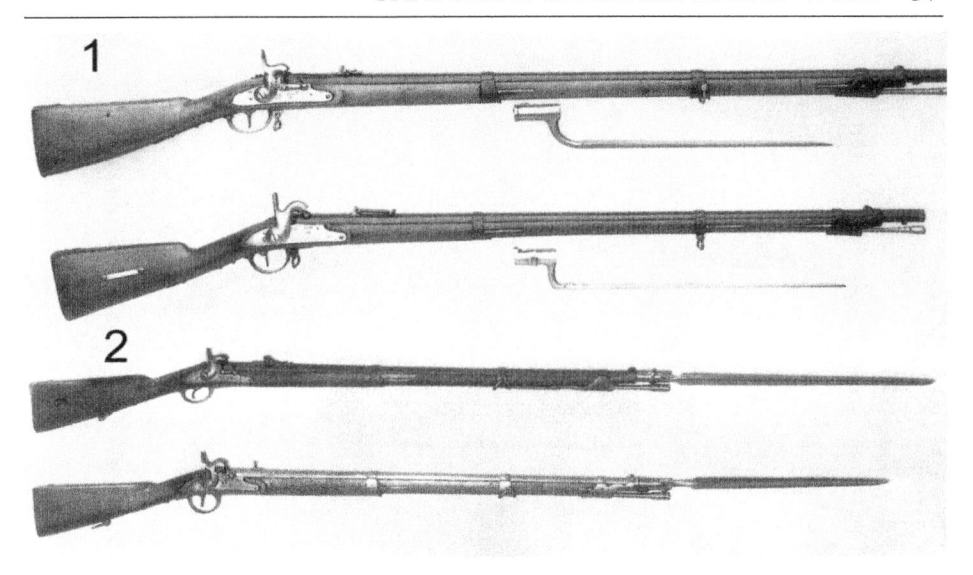

Figure 2.6 Infantry weapons (with permission from Tøjhusmuseet)

1. At the outbreak of the war, the chief infantry weapons were the smoothbore musket model 1822 and model 1828, both types reconfigured to percussion weapons. During the course of the war further smoothbore muskets were purchased in France.

2. The pillar breech rifle model 1848 of Danish construction was not used before 1849. The Danish factory at Ellsinore on Zealand only had a low capacity. In addition to the new rifle, old muskets of model 1831 were reconfigured to become pillar breech rifles. It was not possible to deliver pillar breach rifles to all battalions and only the Chasseur battalions were issued with rifles, thus each of the Chasseur battalions - in addition to smoothbores - possessed 200 rifles.

infantry was equipped with rifles whereas half of the Schleswig Holstein army had rifles. A few of the Prussian units had single shot breech loading rifles, which was the weapon of the Prussian army in 1864. The Prussian and Schleswig Holstein infantry were therefore better equipped than the Danish army.

The Danish cavalry had smoothbore pistols, carbines with flintlocks and sabres. These old flintlock weapons were replaced during the war with percussion pistols and rifles (figure 2.7).

The Schleswig Holstein army used the captured equipment from the depot of Rendsburg. However this was not sufficient and more weapons were purchased both in 1848 and 1849.

The field artillery consisted of smoothbore muzzle-loading cannons. There were two types – the 'solid ball cannon' and the light howitzer (figures 2.8 and 2.9). The 'solid ball cannon' fired massive iron balls whereas the light howitzers used circular shells, which contained an explosive charge. The latter had a primer, which was ignited by an explosion in the gun barrel (Appendix E). The longer the primer the longer it took before the charge of the shell exploded.

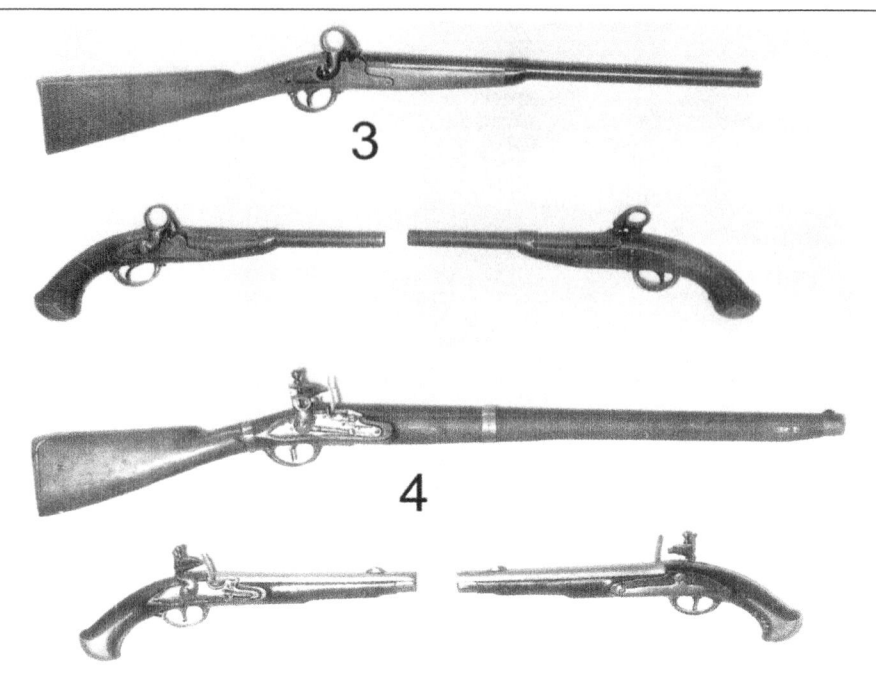

Figure 2.7 Cavalry weapons (with permission from Tøjhusmuseet)

3. Flintlock carbine model 1830 and flintlock pistol model 1806 (both smoothbores) used by the Danish cavalry. As a consequence of the lack of weapons at the outbreak of the war the cavalry were issued these old weapons, however during the war they were replaced with percussion weapons.

Figure 2.8 84 pound light howitzer of 1834 system in siege gun carriage. Maximum range was 3,000 m but effective range was less than 1,000 m.
(with permission from Tøjhusmuseet)

CHAPTER 2: LANDSCAPES AND WARS 39

Figure 2.9 A six pound solid ball gun of the 1834 system in field gun carriage with limber. The effective range was ca. 600 m. The system 1834 was an excellent smoothbore gun which marked the zenith and the end of the smoothbore artillery
(with permission from Tøjhusmuseet)

The 'solid ball cannon' was used for fixed targets and the iron ball was intended to breach obstacles e.g., a brick wall or a massive formation of soldiers. In order to shoot the heavier iron ball a larger charge was necessary and the walls of the barrel in the 'solid ball cannon' were therefore heavier than for a similar howitzer. The howitzers were shooting in a curved trajectory indirectly at targets frequently hidden, whereas the balls exploded on target.

The size of a gun is classified by its calibre. Today it is the diametre of the round but in 1848 it was the weight of the solid ball. The shell was (confusingly) classified as the solid ball with the same diametre despite its weight being less, i.e a 24 pound shell had the same diametre as a 24 pound solid ball but the weight was less than 24 pounds.

Both types of guns could fire grapeshot, a tin with smaller size balls inside. When the grapeshot was fired the tin disintegrated and the balls spread out in front of the cannon. The grapeshot was used if infantry attacked the artillery.

The Danish cannons were made out of iron and constructed after a design by the Danish Colonel J.S. Fibiger. The idea was that a battery should have both types of cannons able to use the same gun carriage. The calibre scale for the artillery was therefore constructed so that the total weight of a solid ball cannon was the same as the total weight of the next highest calibre shell cannon, i.e. a six pound solid ball cannon had the same weight as a 12 pound shell cannon.

In order that each battery could have both types of cannons the Danish artillery was organised in either light batteries with six 6 pound solid ball cannons and two 12 pound shell cannons or heavy batteries with six 12 pound solid ball cannons and two 24 pound shell cannons. When the artillery was fired they were either aiming directly at the target or by an indirect shot where the ball or shell ricocheted on the ground before impact; the restriction being that the ground had to be firm and level and the target larger than with the direct shot.

The cannons were placed in the open or in half cover and generally in the front or between the battalions if placed further back so there was free passage for the shot towards the enemy as it was simply too dangerous to shoot above one's own

Figure 2.10 An espignol with a calibre of 15 mm. The espignols were small rapid firing muzzle-loading weapons. They were loaded with 16 or 32 lead balls with powder charges between. They were ignited in the front and could maintain a fire for several minutes (with permission from Tøjhusmuseet)

units. Due to the primitive signal equipment and methods it was not possible to coordinate the shootings from several batteries unless they were closely arranged.

In 1848 during the rebellion the Schleswig-Holstein army took over the arsenal in Rendsburg and their equipment was therefore the same as for the Danish army. The Prussian army had similar artillery as the Danes.

The Danish army also had an early version of the machine gun, the espignol (figure 2.10), a Danish invention from the war of 1807–14, which were small calibre muzzle-loading weapons with 16 or 32 lead balls with powder charges between. When ignited from the front they shot like 'Roman lights' fire crackers. Hence the espignol would keep up a continuous fire for several minutes. When the shooting was over, the barrel was taken out of the carrier and reloaded behind the front. The shooting range was 125 metres, but by rifling the barrels and using more streamlined bullets the range was extended to 379 metres (this happened in 1849). Three men were required to service the espignol. It was used on several occasions e.g., at Sundeved in May and June 1848 and at last at Friedrichstadt in 1850.

The Navies during the First Schleswig War

The Danish Navy was destroyed and/or captured by the English in 1807. Since that time it had been rebuilt (table 3 and 4) and at the break-out of the war it consisted of seven ships of the line, nine frigates, four corvettes, five brigs and barks, three schooners and six steam ships, in total 34 larger ships with a variable number of guns and crew (figure 2.11). In addition to this the navy had 87 gun barges.

According to the official record (*Generalstaben*) the Royal Danish Navy could muster some 22,000 men of which some 2,000 made up the permanent crew such

Figure 2.11.1 **The Royal Danish Navy - type of ships.** In 1848 the Royal Danish Navy consisted of mostly sailing vessels but steamers were introduced in the 1840s and were important for towing, and the transportation of troops. The Danish army could therefore be moved quickly between different areas, a new tactic that was used optimally. In the front a rowing gun barge and a frigate, behind a ship of the line.

as officers, non-commissioned officers, gunners, carpenters, etc. The rest were conscripted fishermen and sailors of the merchant navy. The naval crew was mostly Danish but according to Holst and Larsen (1888) one third was from Schleswig Holstein and at the rebellion not available. The conscripted were enlisted at the age of 16 and remained on the list until they were 50. These figures cover availability and not the actual crew. In 1848 some 13 ships of various sizes and 16 rowing gun barges were active as well as the transport fleet. The figures of the active crew are listed in table 3. If we add the crew from the transport fleet and the staff in the Copenhagen base the navy had a maximum of 4,000 men in 1848. This figure was increased to between 5,000 and 6,000 men in 1849 when the ships of the line were activated. In 1850 when the peace with the German Confederation and Prussia had been signed the Danish navy probably mustered some 4,000 men. The naval crews in Copenhagen were mostly Danish hence there was no mutiny in the navy.

The main task of the Royal Danish Navy was transport and blockade of the German harbours. At the beginning of the war the steamers showed their value as they could tow several sailing ships and in that way transport the Danish army from Zealand and Funen to Jutland in record time. Later, in connection with army operations from the Island of Als in 1848 and at Frederichia in 1849 the navy played an essential role for the concentration of the army. The German states had no navy hence the Danes totally dominated the sea from the beginning of the war and so the Danish army did not have to protect Zealand and Funen and all the

Figure 2.11.2 The Royal Danish Navy – type of ships. The corvette *Valkyrien* and the paddle steamer *Geiser* chasing Schleswig Holstein paddle steamers outside the river Weser in the North Sea.

Figure 2.12 A rowing gun barge of the dinghy type in action during the attack on Dybbøl 5th June, 1848. This type had 20 oarsmen and the gun directed backwards. The gunboats were very useful in giving the army artillery support during the operations around Sundeved and at Fredericia.

other small islands but could be concentrated on the tasks in Jutland and Schleswig. This was in contrast to the German army which had to use troops for protection of the coasts. The German troops were therefore often scattered, which in certain situations was crucial for the Danish operations.

The Danish blockade of the German North Sea and Baltic harbours damaged the German trading and the financial consequences of this made the war unpopular in parts of Germany.

The navy was divided into three squadrons: the Baltic, the North Sea, and the squadron assisting the army with transport. The Baltic squadron ensured the blockade of the Schleswig harbours and in 1849 it was extended to Prussian harbours in the eastern Baltic, although it was always in reserve for transportation of troops. The North Sea squadron was used for the blockading of the rivers Elbe, Weser and Jade from 1849, resulting in a full blockade of Germany. A small group of minor boats had their base at Fanø Island on the west coast of Jutland, which was not occupied by German troops. These boats made several operations during the war against the Schleswig-Holsteiners' islands off the west coast of Schleswig.

In 1850 when Prussia signed a peace treaty with Denmark pulling out of the war, the naval operations ceased in the North Sea, apart from operations in the shallow waters around the islands of the west coast of Schleswig, and were concentrated on blockading the Schleswig Holstein Baltic coast.

A special chapter in the history of naval operations are the rowing gunbarge actions. The gun barges were rowed by sailors (figure 2.12). There were two types of the so-called Chapman gun barges: one large type with 60 oars and 64 crew and a smaller type called a gun dinghy with 20 oars and 24 crew. The boats were armed with one or two guns and a mix of hand weapons. The gun barges were first used in the war with England in 1807–14. Though they had been improved, the invention of steamboats cast doubts as to their future. Despite these uncertainties during the war of 1848 to 1850 they were used on numerous occasions in connection with the operations at Sundeved where they flanked enemy batteries forcing them to retreat. The boats could only be destroyed by a direct hit, which did occur but were protected from infantry attacks as long as they stayed in deep water. By 1864 they were taken out of service as the more modern rifles and guns made them useless operating near shore.

The larger ships were also used in connection with army operations, (e.g., at the battle at Bov) where three corvettes, a steamer and some gun barges enfiladed the Schleswig-Holstein retreat along the coast to Flensburg and later some of the crew went ashore in Flensburg participating in the last actions of the battle at Bov.

Due to the Danish naval dominance there were no significant battles between large navy units but several engagements between land batteries and the ships. These latter actions demonstrated that sailing ships were not suited for combat with land batteries, which was so tragically shown in the affair at Eckernförde in 1849.

The first steamship in the Danish Navy was the *Kiel* which was bought in 1824. In the following 15 years the navy observed the development of steamships before two more were bought in Britain, *Ægir* and *Hekla*, in 1841 and 1842 respectively. It was then decided to build the steamers in the naval yard in Copenhagen and the first, *Gejser*, was delivered in 1844.

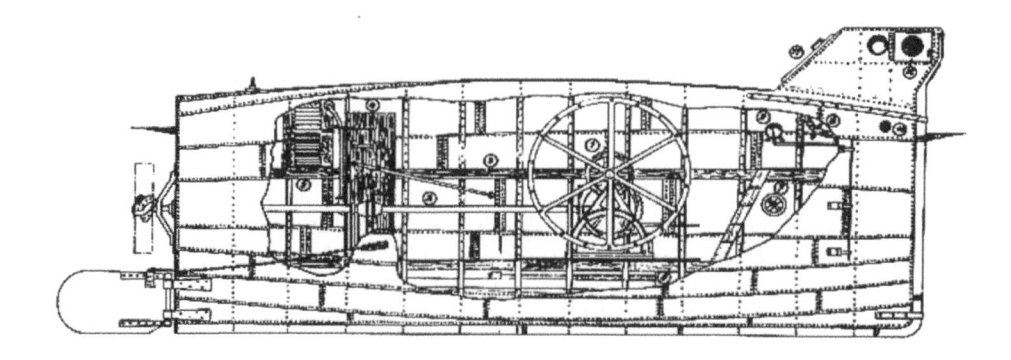

Figure 2.13 *Brandtaucher*, the test submarine of the Schleswig Holstein Navy (Wikipedia)

The Schleswig Holsteiners' did not have a navy at the onset of the war, however in 1850 they had assembled three armed steamships, one schooner and 12 gun barges (table 3). The frigate *Gefion* which was captured at the affair at Eckernförde was refitted and included in the German Confederation navy under the name of *Eckernförde*. It was therefore not kept as part of the Schleswig Holstein armaments, as they were all taken back by the Danes when the Schleswig Holstein army and navy were dissolved in 1851.

One of the Schleswig Holstein steamers was sent with three gun barges through the Eider canal to the west coast islands to protect them from the Danish North Sea squadron.

The steam ship *von der Tann* was operating in the Neustadt bay area near Lübeck with support from two gun barges at Heiligenhafen near the island of Fehmarn. The others were operating from the Kiel area. *von der Tann* was chased by the Danes in July 1850 and escaped to the harbour of Lübeck but had to leave the neutral water and was thereafter grounded and destroyed by the Danish navy on 20th July.

The German Confederation had three steamship frigates, four steamship corvettes and a sailing frigate. These ships had an encounter outside Elben with the Danish Navy.

The Schleswig Holstein Navy also tried to construct a submarine called the *Brandtaucher* (figure 2.13), which was completed in Rendsburg and launched in Kiel in December 1850. The engineer for this novelty was Wilhelm Bauer (1822–75), a Bavarian non-commissioned artillery officer in the Schleswig Holstein army. He had observed the dominance of the Danish navy and wanted a tool to break the blockade. He proposed the solution to the provisional government in January 1850 and after a model was built and tested the full-sized submarine was constructed at the steel factory in Rendsburg. It was eight metres long and two to three metres wide. It had a displacement of ca. 30 tons, a crew of three men, one for navigating and two for operating the tread wheel which ran the propeller. Unfortunately it sank when it was launched in the water. After it had been raised, it was made ready for a second trial on 1st February 1851. Bauer and two men dived in the vessel but it leaked and they had to escape by opening the hatch when the pressure had equalized with the outside and swim to the surface.

After the war, Bauer then tried to convince other nations to build submarines, including Great Britain, which liked the idea and gave him funding. However, controversy with the British forced him to leave the project before the vessel was completed. Eventually he worked in Russia during the Crimean war and constructed a third submarine. This was more successful but eventually it went down with its crew.

The *Brandtaucher* was salvaged in 1887 and is now on exhibition in the Dresden War Museum. It is interesting to note that the submarine has been ignored in the early Danish literature on the war. But it was the first submarine in northern Europe even though it was more a curiosity than an influence on the war.

Chapter 3

1848

The Battle at Bov

At the onset of the Schleswig Holstein rebellion six battalions of infantry and three dragoon regiments joined the Schleswig Holstein army. Since most of the officers were Danish, they and a few of the Schleswig-Holstein officers loyal to the Danish King declined to participate. Therefore the Prince of Nör, who had been chosen as the commanding officer of the Schleswig Holstein Army, asked the Prussian King to urgently supply officers.

King Friedrich Wilhelm of Prussia agreed and immediately dispatched 20 officers with more to follow. The Prince also called in six classes of the reserve. In addition to the regulars some volunteer units were also formed. Therefore when his army moved into the Duchy of Schleswig in early April it consisted of two brigades, two mounted regiments and two field batteries. The army was supplied from the captured Danish depots in Rendsburg.

Due to the short notice it was not possible to produce a special uniform for the Schleswig Holstein army, thus the soldiers were mostly dressed in Danish uniforms, although they avoided wearing the red coats. The Prince's army moved north to Flensburg and took position at the village of Bov immediately north of Flensburg (map 4). At the same time the Prussian and other German troops were assembling in Holstein though they were not yet prepared for action.

On 25th March, A. F. Tscherning took over as Secretary of War in Denmark, and he was clearly the right man for the job. He was originally trained as an officer but had mostly worked as an engineer. He was used to organising and leading projects.

Anton Frederik Tscherning's (1795–1874) family was from Silesia in Germany and had emigrated to Denmark in 1600 (figure 3.1). Tscherning had grown up in *Frederiksværk* on Zealand where his father was inspector in the powder and gun factory.

Anton entered the army at a young age and became a cadet in 1810. In 1813 he was Lieutenant with the army in Holstein but did not participate in the fighting. After the war Tscherning was with the units of the Danish army in France together with the allied troops. Tscherning managed to get to Paris and study artillery. When he returned in 1818 he worked as a volunteer for his father in the factory. Despite an offer from the King he declined to take over after his father as leader of the factory. In 1828 he was, together with the later General and Secretary of War, C. F. Hansen, in Greece as observers with the French expeditionary corps during the Greek War of Independence.

In 1829 he returned and became teacher at the school of artillery in Denmark. Due to his liberal views, he managed to get on the wrong side of the royal regime and was sent out of the country, in reality expelled, though in 1838 he was allowed

CHAPTER 3: 1848   47

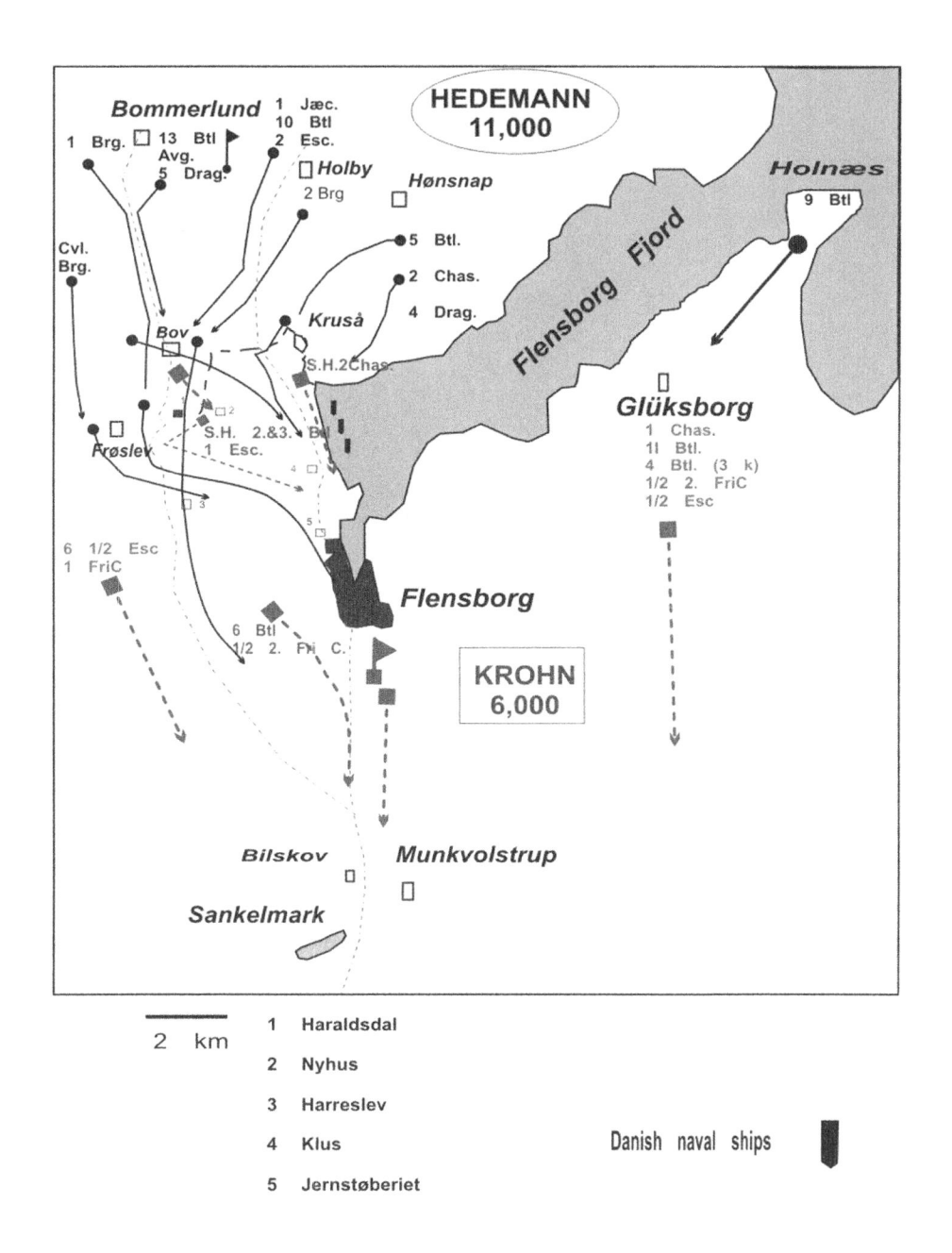

Map 4 The Battle at Bov 9th April 1848

Figure 3.1 **Anton Frederik Tscherning (1795–1874)** became secretary of war when the new Danish government was formed on 25th March 1848. In November 1848 he resigned as he considered the division of Schleswig as the only possible solution to the conflict. This was in contrary to Fredrik VII's thinking. Tscherning then participated as a member of the Danish parliament until 1866 where he withdrew from public life. He was married to a cousin, Eleonora Cristine Lützow who survived him until 1890.

to return. He wanted to resign from the army but this was denied. At this juncture, he worked as an engineer in France until he could finally resign from the army, which finally occurred in 1842. He returned to Denmark and worked as an architect and engineer. In the same period he started his liberal political career.

When appointed, Tscherning was not part of the military hierarchy and was therefore free to choose his commanding officers based on qualification. His first task was to appoint a Supreme Commander for the army as it was clear that the current army generals were not suited for war. His choice was Colonel Hedemann (figure 3.2) with Captain Læssøe as Chief of Staff (figure 3.3).

Hans Christoph Frederik Hedemann (1792–1859) was born in Flensburg and became a cadet in 1803. He then worked in the army and was slowly promoted until in 1842 he became Lieutenant Colonel.

Læssøe was an old friend of Tscherning, they had both participated in the same liberal political work. Verner Hans Frederik Abrahamson Læssøe (1811–1850) was born in Copenhagen and joined the army at an early age. In 1842 he delivered a proposal to the military commission working on the new army re-formation. The same year he wrote some critical notes on the army in the newspapers which were not well received by the high command. At that time young roosters were sent abroad to cool down and so was Læssøe. He visited several European countries where he studied military organisation. During the time

Figure 3.2 **Hans Christoph Frederik Hedemann (1792-1859)** was born in Flensburg and became cadet in 1803. Tscherning offered him the Supreme Command of the Danish Army in 1848 and he and Læssøe commanded the army until 25th July 1848, when he was sacked. Hedemann was very disappointed and surprised. Many officers supported Hedemann and delivered supporting letters to the ministry. He was then sent to Copenhagen where he was in charge of a military commission until he retired in 1854. Five years later he died, totally blind.

abroad he was promoted to Captain. Before and after his travels he participated in the topographic mapping of Denmark which at that time was under the supervision of the army.

It was Tscherning's idea that Læssøe should be the *de facto* leader and Hedemann should only play the role as the leading officer. There is no record that tells us what Hedemann felt about this organisation or if he knew anything about it.

The army equipment stored in Rendsburg was captured by the Schleswig Holsteins; hence the Danish army needed replacements for these and a large number of muskets and rifles as well as guns were bought from other countries.

The Danish army was transported to the island of Als in the south of Jutland. The transport was carried out in the main by using sailing ships towed by steamboats. In this way the movement of troops was carried out in record time and by the beginning of April the army, totalling 11,000 men, had moved from Als and gathered north of Flensburg.

As a diversion, a small taskforce was landed on 7th April at Holdnæs, east of Flensburg. These tactics were successful as the Schleswig Holstein army had to send two battalions and half a squadron to Glüksburg as a defence against the task force.

50 FIRST SCHLESWIG HOLSTEIN WAR

Figure 3.3 **Verner Hans Frederik Abrahamson Læssøe (1811–1850)** was born in Copenhagen and joined the army as a young man. In 1848 he was promoted to Chief of Staff by Tscherning. He had a significant influence on the army operations in 1848. When General Hedemann was removed as Supreme Command. Læssøe continued under General Krogh. However in 1849 he also had to leave the staff. He was then promoted to Lieutenant Colonel and commanded the 12. Light Battalion. Læssøe was killed in action at the battle of Isted in 1850 when he was commanding the vanguard of the 2nd Division.

The Danish army was organised into two divisions: The 'North Jutland' division was under the command of General Hedemann consisting of three infantry brigades, a cavalry brigade, a reserve of one infantry battalion, a dragoon regiment and artillery. The 'Schleswig Flank' division was under the command of Colonel Schleppegrell. It consisted of five battalions, and one and a half squadrons of dragoons and artillery.

The landscape around Flensburg and east of the main road (Army Road) is hilly and cut by the valley of the Kruså River. An attacking army from the north has to cross the river at Kruså and Nyhus or outflank the enemy positions by using the main road west of Flensburg (map 4). The deputy commanding officer, General Krohn, of the Schleswig Holstein Army (the commanding officer Prince of Nör was still in Rendsburg) was well aware that his men could be surrounded. His problem was that his army was divided due to the presence of the Danish taskforce at Holdnæs. He requested permission to withdraw, which the Prince of Nör denied as he was under pressure to initiate the fighting in the Duchy of Schleswig by the provisional government of Schleswig Holstein. They wanted to emphasise that the fighting was also about the Duchy of Schleswig rather than only Holstein.

Figure 3.4 The battle at Bov - Captain Hegermann Lindencrone of the 3rd Chasseur Battalion is carried away dead. Note: the skirmish line has taken cover behind a fence. These were made out of rocks and covered by bushes. They are a common element of the landscape both in Denmark and Schleswig. They were often used as cover in the various battles. The 3rd Chasseur Battalion was part of the Vanguard of the Danish army and had Lieutenant Colonel Magius as CO.

The Danish Supreme Command had indeed planned to surround the enemy and so it was decided that the majority of the Danish army should move along the main road while the rest situated north-east of Kruså should hold back and only observe the units of the Schleswig Holstein Army placed at Kruså.

On the morning of 9th April, 1848 at 8.45 hrs in sunshine the vanguard of the Danish army advanced along the main road towards the village of Bov where they encountered two companies of the Schleswig Holstein 2nd Battalion. The fighting at Bov (figure 3.4) lasted for half an hour during which time the Danish units forced the Schleswig Holsteiners to retreat towards the south-east.

Half of Colonel Schleppegrell's 'Schleswig Flank' division advanced towards Bov at 9.00 hrs and when the Division reached Bov, Schleppegrell commanded his chasseur battalion to take a position east of the village. The battalion became involved in some minor skirmishing with the Schleswig Holstein units and at 11.00 hrs it continued its advance. In response the Schleswig Holstein units retreated to Flensburg without any further resistance. The retreat was actually a misunderstanding between the Schleswig Holstein officers.

Count Baudissin, the commanding officer of the Schleswig Holstein 2nd Battalion and two companies of the 3rd Battalion at Nyhus and Bov observed that his left flank was open. He therefore ordered Major Kint to take up position with his 2nd Battalion between Nyhus and Haraldsdal near the Army road. Major Kint moved forward with his troops, but when he observed the Danish troops (Schleppegrel's 10th Battalion and 1st Chasseur battalion) he ordered his troops to retreat to the hills north of Flensburg. There he got orders to continue the retreat.

Figure 3.5 During the retreat from Kruså the Schleswig Holstein 2. Chasseur Battalion was pursued by parts of the Flank Division. The road from Kruså runs along the coast to Flensburg. On the fjord is a Danish frigate, steamer and some gun barges that were shooting at the Schleswig Holstein troops withdrawing, and also by mistake at the pursuing Danish troops. Both parties had similar uniforms in the first battle of the war, hence the error.

He informed Count Baudissin about the change. Baudissin could now see that his flank was completely open and he could therefore do nothing else than also order his troops to go back.

The Danish mounted brigade had also moved along the main road and had reached Frøslev sand while the fighting at Bov took place. During the advance it had learned that enemy units were seen south and south-east of Frøslev. It was therefore decided to await the arrival of the 1st Brigade commanded by Colonel Bülow. Upon arrival Colonel Bülow commanded his brigade to attack despite an exhausting march of his troops during the morning. At 11.30 hrs he moved on and despite some severe resistance, the Schleswig Holstein units were forced back from Harreslev.

Colonel Schleppegrell's units arrived at Harreslev after the fighting had ceased and therefore decided to continue and take the southern part of Flensburg.

At 12.00 hrs the Danish units at Kruså observed that the Schleswig Holstein units were retreating so they took pursuit. During the fighting a corvette, a steamer and a gun barge of the Danish Royal Navy had sailed into Flensburg fjord and when they saw the enemy units retreating along the coast road they enfiladed the coast with their guns (figure 3.5).

At the same time the Prince of Nör had arrived in Flensburg and as soon as he was briefed about the situation he commanded his army to retreat but this message was not conveyed to the units at Kruså. The retreating Schleswig Holstein units from Kruså discovered, when they reached the hills north of Flensburg, that the town had been evacuated by the other part of the Schleswig Holstein army. They

Figure 3.6 During the last phase of the battle around Flensburg a squadron of the Danish Cavalry under Captain Sauerbrey attacked the Schleswig Holstein Chasseurs who were retreating to Flensburg.

were then attacked by Colonel Büllow's battalions who reached the outskirts of Flensburg at the same time (figure 3.6). Other Danish battalions under the command of Colonel Rye moved into the southern part of Flensburg and blocked the southern road. A considerable number of Schleswig Holstein soldiers were captured. The naval ships had landed some of its crew in the harbour who participated in the last part of the fighting.

The Danish mounted brigade attempted to stop the retreat of the remnant Schleswig Holstein battalions, which first assembled on the hills south of Flensburg, but due to difficult terrain and to a long and exhausting day for both men and horses the mounted brigade were not able to interfere in the Schleswig Holstein retreat. The Prince of Nör who had ordered the retreat, had hoped to be able to stop at Isted and present some kind of resistance. His army was, however, too demoralised for any such thing. Instead his army continued south to the Eider River. He only left skirmishers north of the river.

The Schleswig Holstein losses during the battle were 177 dead and wounded and 923 taken as prisoners of war. The Danish losses were much smaller, 94 dead and wounded and no prisoners.

The Battle at the town of Schleswig

The Danish Army moved through the town of Schleswig and took up positions south and west of the city in a line from Bustrup to Tiergarten (map 5). The skirmish line was positioned between the town of Schleswig and the river Eider. A minor unit was stationed at Mysunde with a company in a forward position at

Figure 3.7 **Friederich Heinrich Ernst Wrangel (1784–1877)** was born in Stettin in Prussia as a son of a Prussian Major General.

Eckernförde. During the next days the Danish army tested the German positions with forward patrol activity but only encountered the German skirmish line at Eckernförde, Wittensee and Sorgbrücke in the east.

At the same time the German and Prussian troops were assembling at Rendsburg. On 21st April the Prussian General Wrangel arrived and took over the command of the entire army.

Friedrich Heinrich Ernst Wrangel (1784–1877) was born in Kolber in Prussia as a son of a Prussian Major General (figure 3.7). He joined the army early on and participated in the Napoleonic wars as a cavalry officer. He distinguished himself in the battle at Heilsberg in 1807 and later in the Prussian war of liberation from 1813 to 1815. In 1814 he was promoted to Colonel and regiment commander. In 1834 he had advanced to General. During the armistice later in 1848 his troops were used in Berlin to suppress the remaining opposition to the King. He was promoted to Field Marshall in 1856 and in 1864 given the task to lead the combined Prussian–Austrian troops who invaded Denmark. He was then at the age of 80 and functioned more as a public figure than the real leader of the two armies.

General Wrangel had 12,000 Prussian soldiers, 10,000 from the German Confederation Army and 9,000 Schleswig Holstein troops under his command. However, the contribution from the Confederation was not assembled yet at Rendsburg. Nevertheless he decided to attack and on 23rd April he commanded his troops to advance north. The attack plan had been worked out prior to his

CHAPTER 3: 1848   55

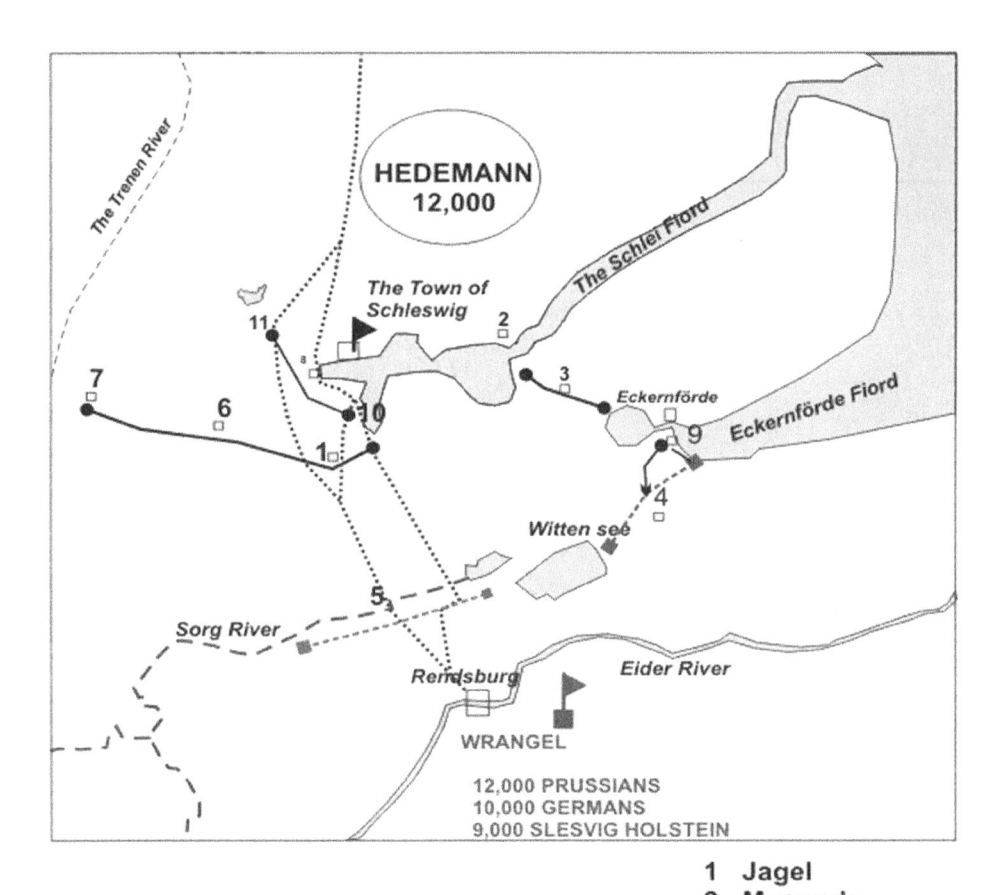

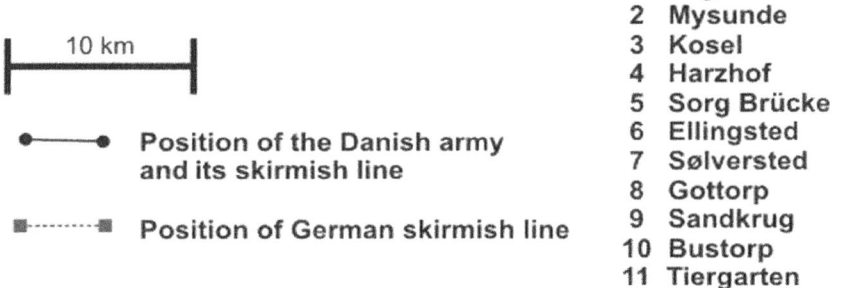

1 Jagel
2 Mysunde
3 Kosel
4 Harzhof
5 Sorg Brücke
6 Ellingsted
7 Sølversted
8 Gottorp
9 Sandkrug
10 Bustorp
11 Tiergarten

●——● Position of the Danish army and its skirmish line

■┄┄┄┄■ Position of German skirmish line

Map 5a The battle at the town of Schleswig April 1848
(1): Skirmishes 15th–23rd April 1848

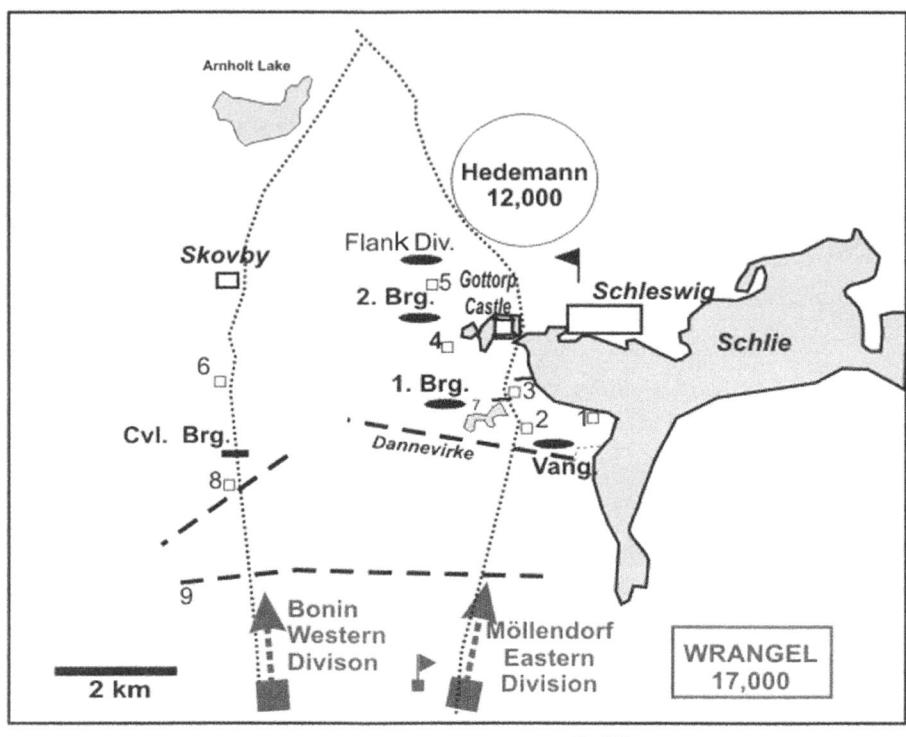

56 FIRST SCHLESWIG HOLSTEIN WAR

1 Hadeby
2 Bustorp
3 Friedrichberg
4 Annetenhöhe and Pulvermühle brickwork
5 Tiergarten
6 Hysby
7 Bustorp Dam
8 Ll. Dannevirke
9 Kovirke

Map 5b The battle at the town of Schleswig April 1848
(2): The German advance 23rd April 1848

arrival and he just approved it. The weather on this day was sunny but changed to rain during the night.

In total 17,000 men, Prussian and from Schelswig Holstein, moved in two divisions: the western under command of General Bonin and the eastern under General Möllendorff. General Bonin commanded seven battalions, 10 squadrons and guns. The Schleswig Holstein units under the command of the Prince of Nör (apart from the voluntary battalion) followed General Möllendorf's division, which took the road from Rendsburg via Beckendorf to the town of Schleswig.

The western division took the road over Sorg Brücke and Kosel. The plan was that the army should advance to Dannevirke and assemble as one unit before any further action.

Both columns began the march between six and seven in the morning and at 10.00 hrs the vanguard of the eastern division had reached the southern arm of the Dannevirke. They found that this and the northern arm were not defended and therefore continued towards Bustrup in order to surround the Danish skirmishers who had been observed earlier.

The Danish Supreme Command had in the meantime received reports about the German advance and ordered all Danish troops onto high alert. In response the Danish vanguard moved from Friedrichberg to Bustrup and Risbjerg where it met the German vanguard, which was immediately forced back to Dannevirke. A fierce battle now developed where the Danes were able to hold the Prussian battalions back as they came into the battle zone from the rear (figure 3.8).

Around noon the Danish Supreme Command decided to have two battalions of the 1st Brigade go on the offensive. This was conducted over some wet areas just

Figure 3.8 Episode from the Battle at Schleswig 23rd April 1848 ca.11.30 hrs. Lieutenant Glud's two guns were positioned just south of Friederichberg at the main road from Bustorp. His guns were able to maintain a steady fire against the German troops despite heavy fire from their opponents.

58 FIRST SCHLESWIG HOLSTEIN WAR

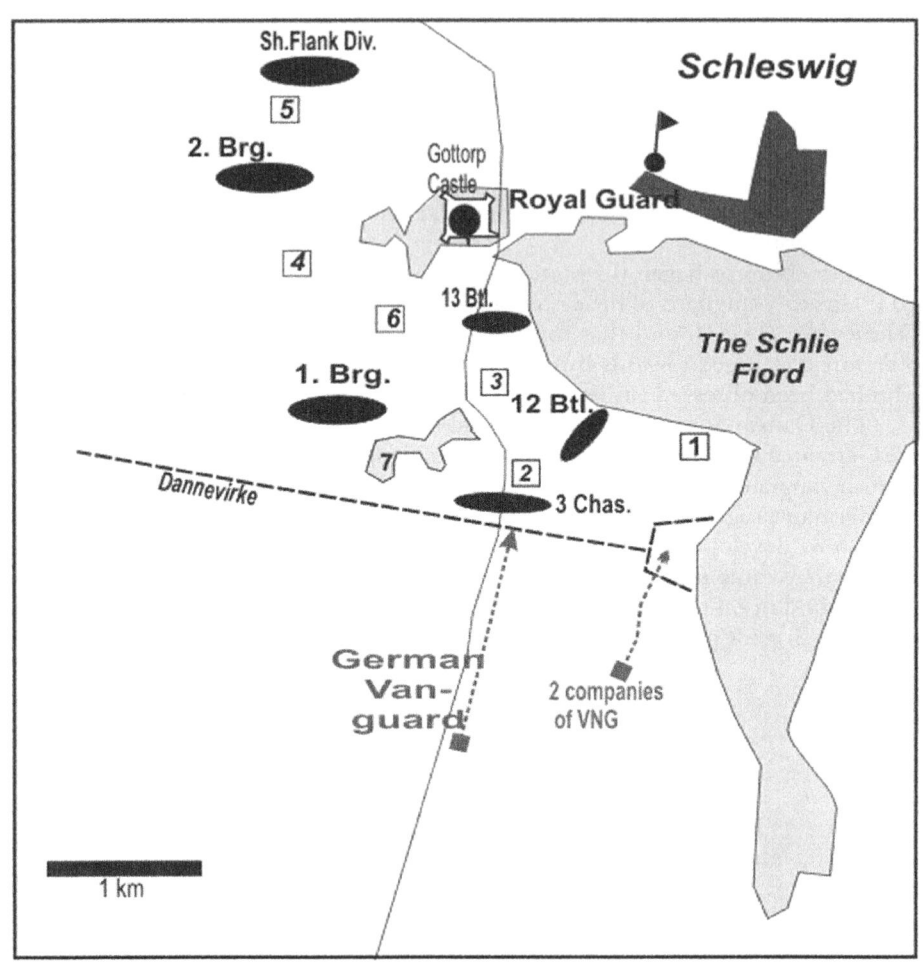

1 Hadeby 3 Friedrichberg 5 Tiergarten
2 Bustorp 4 Annetenhöhe and Pulvermühle brickwork 6 Erdberenberg
7 Bustorp Dam

Map 6a The battle at the town of Schleswig April 1848
(3): 10:00–12:00 hours

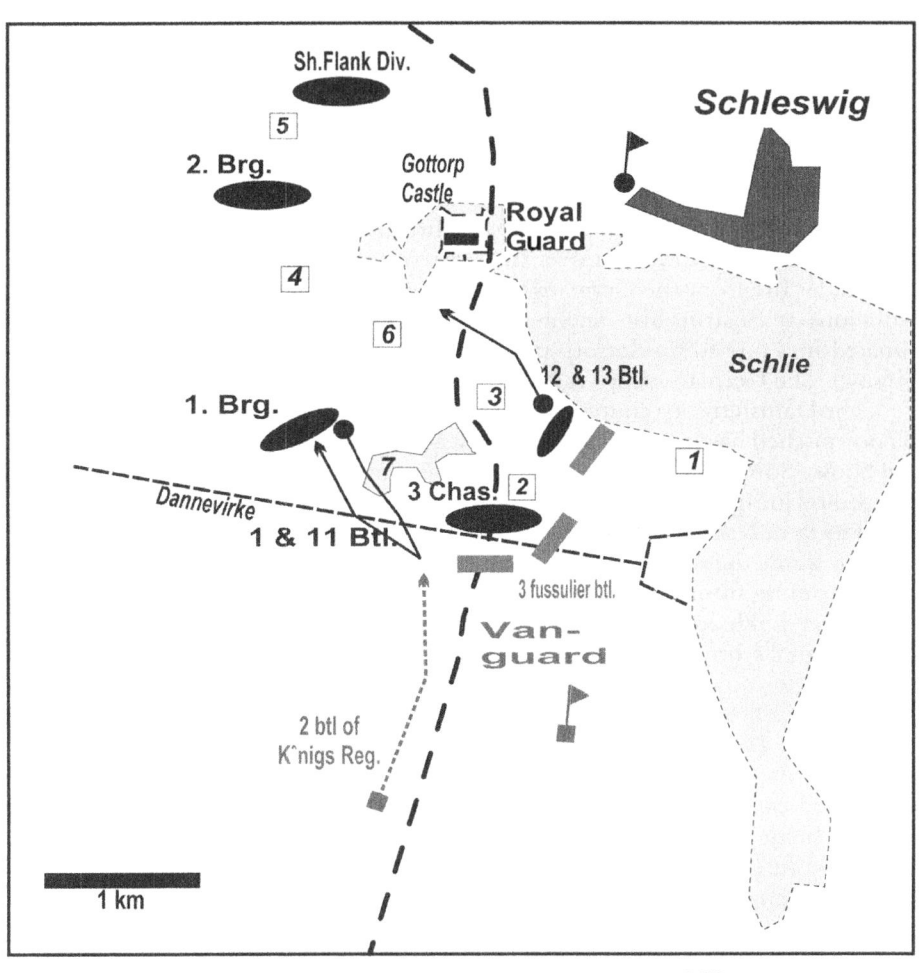

CHAPTER 3: 1848   59

1 Hadeby
2 Bustorp
3 Friedrichberg
4 Annetenhöhe and Pulvermühle brickwork
5 Tiergarten
6 Erdberenberg
7 Bustorp Dam

Map 6b The battle at the town of Schleswig April 1848
(4): 12:00–13:30 hours

south of Lake Bustrup (map 6). Simultaneously the 13th Battalion was moved forward to support the Danish vanguard. The attack was conducted in a resolute manner, which threatened the Prussian troops.

General Wrangel, the CO of all the German troops who had now arrived at the front, sent a message back to hurry up the units which were straggling behind on the road. The messenger reached General Bonin's rearguards of his western division, who immediately turned around and by forced marched reached the front at Bustrup and participated in the attack on the Danish troops. This change was never communicated to General Bonin so he continued his march towards the north along the planned road.

The two Danish Battalions of the first brigade under the command of Colonel Bülow were forced to retreat over the same wet areas they had attacked but were now under fire from the Germans which resulted in some casualties. The Danish battalions at Bustrup also retreated so that at 13.30 hrs the Danish army was situated in a line from Gottorp castle to the farm at Annetenhöe and further to Hysbye. The German troops followed and took the farm.

The Danish troops counter-attacked and shortly after recaptured the farm in a bloody pitched battle, which at a certain stage took place from room to room inside the house. Some of the German officers were nearly captured or killed and only escaped by jumping out of the windows.

The farm is situated on a high point west of the castle Gottorp. There are steep slopes towards the south and the area is in an ideal position defensively towards an enemy coming from the south.

General Hedemann of the Danish Army now commanded Colonel Schleppegrell's brigade to advance. As they reached Ziegelei the 10th Battalion continued to move forward as support of the left flank of the troops fighting at Annetenhöe. The battalion immediately encountered resistance from the German troops of the 2nd Königs Regiment resulting in a gap in the front, which was then covered by the 9th Battalion. The front was stabilised and General Hedemann now considered expanding the attack and therefore commanded the 2nd Brigade to advance (map 7).

The Prussian General Bonin, as mentioned earlier, had not been informed that his rearguard had deviated from its planned route and was now fighting to the east at Gottorp. He therefore continued his march towards the north to the Kurgraven, an arm of the old Dannevirke rampart, where he stopped. It was here that he became aware that his rearguard had disappeared. He also noticed movement of the Danish troops and as he did not have his entire division ready he decided not to continue. However, a messenger from General Wrangel commanded him to resume the march along the main road. In response, he sent a messenger to the rear to investigate where his rearguard had disappeared to. He believed that they could not be far away.

The messenger did not meet the rearguard but instead found the Prince of Nör and his Schleswig Holstein army. The Prince in return sent two battalions and ½ Chasseur battalion and some guns to support General Bonin. However, due to the misunderstanding General Bonin's division did not get into battle that day apart from some skirmishing with the Danish cavalry (figure 3.9) and the Germans

CHAPTER 3: 1848   61

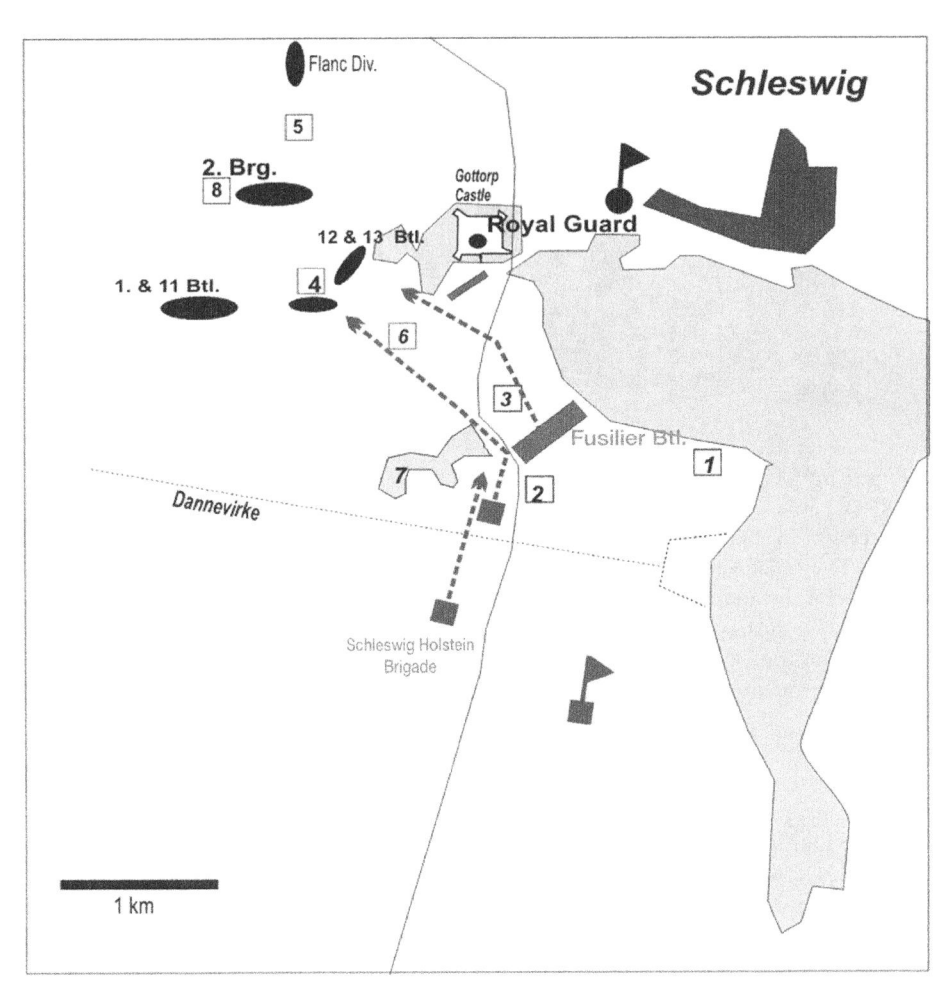

1 Hadeby
2 Bustorp and Risbjerg
3 Friedrichberg
4 Annetenhöle and Pulvermühle brickpit

5 Tiergarten
6 Erdberenberg
7 Bustorp Dam
8 Ziegelei

Map 7   The battle at the town of Schleswig April 1848
(5): after 13:30 hours

Figure 3.9 Captain Würtzen's attack on the Prussian troops near Hysby 23rd April 1848. The attack was conducted in order to save a couple of Danish guns. The move was successful in that the Prussian troops were halted and the Danish guns were able to escape. The squadron was attacking units of the western Prussian Division on the 'Army road'. After the attack the squadron retreated along the road. The Prussian soldiers had taken cover during the first phase of the attack behind the fences along the road. The retreat of the Danish squadron resulted in significant losses, in that 40 of the 180 men-strong squadron were killed or wounded. Würtzen's horse was shot but he managed to escape.

therefore lost the advantage of their superiority in number of troops as only some 12,000 men participated in the fighting at Bustrup.

The Danish Royal Guard at Gottorp Castle received a message that German troops had crossed the Schlie fjord and were now present in the eastern part of Schleswig town. The CO for the Royal Guard, Colonel Juhl, therefore ordered a retreat. There was an attempt to destroy the embankment which connects Friedrichberg and the castle but as the powder was wet this was not accomplished. The retreat thus was done silently. When General Hedemann found out about the retreat he immediately commanded the Guard to return to the castle. Colonel Juhl had also discovered that the presence of German troops in his rear was false and the guard had therefore already returned. Fortunately for them the Prussians had not observed the retreat and therefore not taken the castle.

The time was now 17.00 hrs and the sun was setting (map 7). It would soon be too dark for fighting. The Danes watched as the German reinforcement grew during the day. The Schleswig Holstein army under the Prince of Nör (excluding the troops sent to General Bonin) were now also in the fighting line. General Bonin's troops were on the march again.

The Danish Supreme Command ordered a general retreat that commenced on the western flank and was subsequently followed by the other battalions. The Danish Mounted Brigade had operated along the western main road with some

Figure 3.10 The 2nd Chasseur battalion under the command of Lieutenant Colonel Styrup fighting during the retreat from Schleswig at Oversø on 24th April 1848. Two of the battalion companies were surrounded and captured. Styrup was mortally wounded. In the last phase of the fighting two of the battalions had retreated to a boggy area in order to avoid cavalry attack. The battalion was able to delay the Prussian troops' movement towards the north, making it possible for the Danish troops in Flensburg to gather and retreat northwards unharmed despite the confusion in Flensburg. Note that all the soldiers are wearing field caps. N.P. Jensen, later Colonel, participated in this battle and was captured by the Prussians. He mentions in his memoirs that the soldiers on the ship during the trip from Zealand to Jutland were throwing their shakoes into the water. Therefore when they arrived to the island Als only part of the battalion was wearing the shako. Styrup therefore commanded everybody to wear the field cap. 2nd Chasseur Battalion was therefore the first unit in 1848 where all soldiers wore the field cap.

minor skirmishing with General Bonin's troops and it also retreated during the afternoon. The army continued the retreat to Isted and Arnholt Lake where it camped for the night. The pioneer units had already prepared some defences at this place. The Danish skirmish line at Mysunde was evacuated by boats.

The Prussian General Wrangel had also commanded his troops to camp for the night.

The Danish Supreme Command decided during the night to continue the retreat to Flensburg. With over 700 casualties, the Danes had suffered heavily compared to the Schleswig Holstein Army, who had incurred less than 500 losses. Some skirmishing at Mysunde with the Danish troops stationed there and the Schleswig Holstein volunteer battalions who had been able to cross the fjord with a platoon, suggested that the Danish positions were about to be surrounded. Furthermore there had been some losses, especially of officers, so the idea of resisting the German army at Isted was not considered to be a good one.

Figure 3.11 **Christian Frederik Hansen (1788–1873)** was born in Ellsinore. He originally studied law at Copenhagen University but after having obtained a degree in law in 1806 he joined the army. Like many of his officer colleagues he participated in the Napoleonic war and in 1803 was promoted to lieutenant. In 1848 he was permanent under-secretary to Tscherning. He was not very cooperative with the Parliament and therefore in 1851 he resigned as secretary of war. He returned to office as part of a new government in 1852. As he could not get approval for his military budget from the Parliament he obtained it through unconstitutional methods. He was therefore tried in 1855 but not sentenced. In 1854 the government resigned and he withdrew to his estate. However in 1864 he was called in again as secretary of war in the last phase of the war with Prussia and Austria. The peace treaty was soon after signed and his task was to demobilise the army. In 1865 he withdrew from public service.

During the days before the German and Prussian armies moved into the town of Schleswig there had been an exchange of sharp diplomatic messages between the United Kingdom and Prussia. The Danish government had learned about this and hoped that a war between Denmark and Prussia could be avoided. Secretary of War Tscherning submitted a message to the Supreme Command on the morning of 23rd April, which demanded that the army avoid aggressive action but of course make a firm resistance in case of an attack. The message did not reach General Hedemann before he was on his way to Flensburg. By that time the message had become obsolete as hostilities had already been initiated by the Prussians. Despite the Prussian aggression General Hedemann having then received the message from Tscherning, decided to stop in Flensburg as he assumed that the Prussians would not advance further.

CHAPTER 3: 1848   65

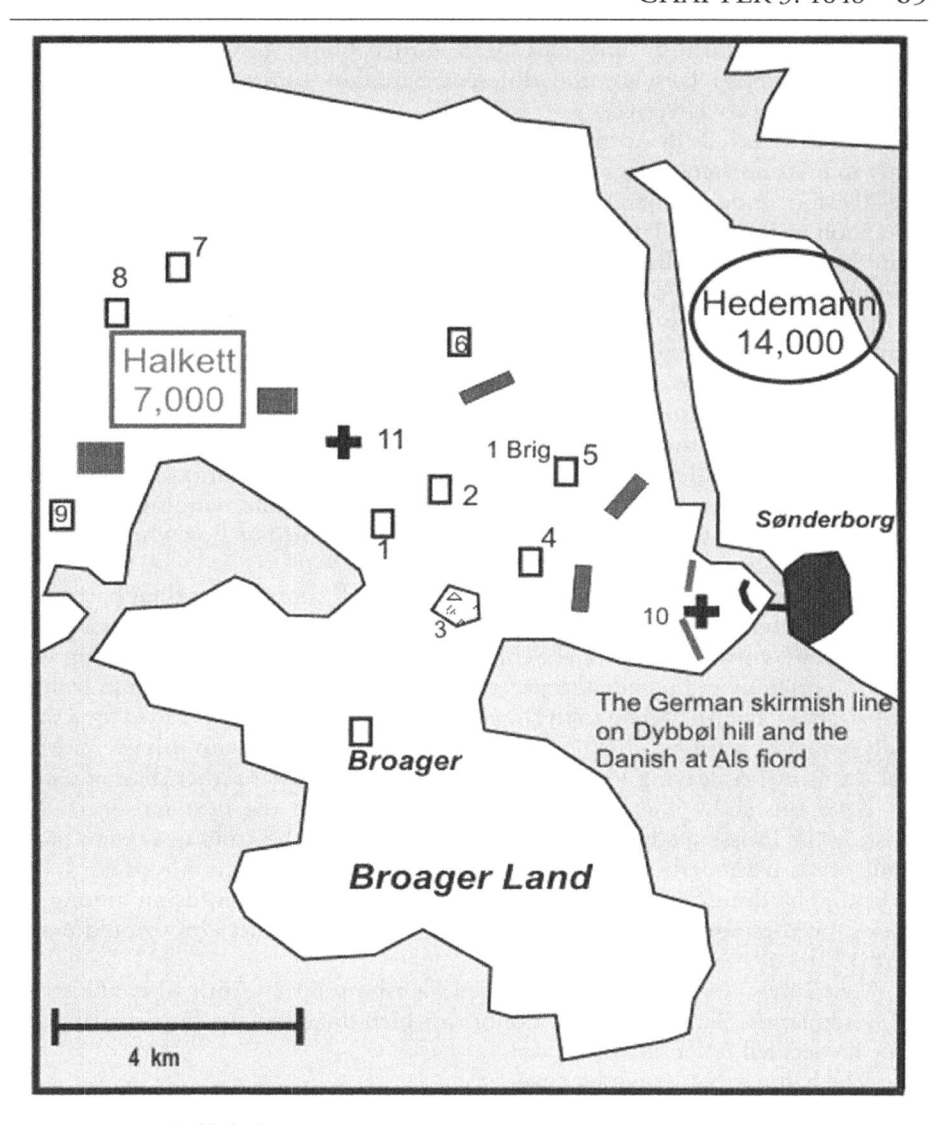

1 Nybøl
2 Stenderup
3 Bøffel Kobbel Wood
4 Dybbøl
5 Ragebøl

6 Vestre Sottrup
7 Ullerup
8 Avnbøl
9 Gråsten
10 Dybbøl Mølle
11 Nybøl Mølle

Map 8 Sundeved 28th May 1848 - situation before the battle

A Danish skirmish line had been posted south of Flensburg. Due to misunderstandings between the different battalion commanders the skirmish guard was not very effective.

The next day, 24th April, the Prussian General Wrangel expected the Danish army to offer resistance after the battle at the town of Schleswig. He commanded the division under General Bonin to march northwards on the 24th. By the afternoon they reached Oversø where its vanguard immediately attacked the Danish 2nd Chasseur Battalion (figure 3.10). The battle continued for two hours during which time the commanding officer of the Danish Chasseur Battalion was mortally wounded with two of the companies surrounded and captured before the remaining Danish companies of the battalion retreated. The other part of the Danish skirmish line was utterly taken by surprise and hurried back to Flensburg.

At 17.00 hrs a group of the Danish mounted skirmishers reached Flensburg spreading panic to the soldiers in the town. For the next few hours there was confusion with soldiers searching for their equipment and units and then once found fleeing northwards. However after some time the commanding officers got their soldiers back under control and the army assembled at Bov where it stayed during the night.

Colonels Bülow and Schleppegrell both had full control over their battalions, positioning them south and north of Flensburg. Remarkably Captain Læssøe, the chief of staff, convinced Colonel Schleppegrell to move back into Flensburg with the 9th Battalion and parade the streets with the military band playing in front of the battalion. They marched to the town central square where it paraded for a short while before retreating to the north. Captain Læssøe's point with this exercise was that the army was leaving Flensburg in a controlled manner rather than in panic.

After this show it was decided to continue north the next day instead of resisting the Prussian advance at Bov. The majority of the army now went to the island of Als at Sønderborg, while a smaller mostly mounted unit moved north into Jutland. The decision was made based on the fatigue and confusion among the troops. Furthermore it was now a given fact that the German army would march north.

Germany's General Wrangel reached Flensburg on 25 April where he set up his headquarters. Since he was in doubt in which direction the Danish army had gone he decided to let his troops rest.

The battle at Schleswig was over.

The German losses were 423 dead and wounded whereas 54 were captured by the Danish. The Danes had 326 dead and wounded but 526 taken as prisoners of war.

Sundeved, 28th and 29th May 1848

After the battle at the town of Schleswig the main part of the Danish troops were stationed on the island of Als (map 8). The task was now to build the army to a larger size with the reserves which had been called in.

By that time the German army was double the size of the Danish and a direct confrontation was not advisable. The immediate task was to reorganise. Secretary of War Tscherning therefore summoned General Hedemann and the bulk of the army to Funen to undertake the reorganisation.

Ten battalions, one squadron and some artillery would defend the island. Colonel Hansen took over as CO for this force. Christian Frederik Hansen (1788–1873) was born in Elsinore (figure 3.11). He originally studied law at Copenhagen University but after having obtained a degree in 1806 he joined the army. As with many of his officer colleagues he participated in the Napoleonic Wars and was in 1803 promoted to lieutenant. He was with the allied occupation force in France after the war. In 1842 he had promoted to colonel in the supreme staff. He was one of the people who drove the army reorganisation in 1842. In 1848 he became permanent under-secretary to Tscherning. C.F. Hansen was, contrary to Tscherning's liberalism, very conservative and in opposition to democratic political thinking. He however, completely agreed with compulsory military service and believed that it was the duty of every person to defend country and king. He was a very self-willed person.

He was sent to Als to investigate the rumours that had reached Copenhagen concerning the panic in Flensburg. The Colonel had been given a power of attorney by Tscherning to act on his behalf. He used this power to take the command on Als. This intrigue made the relations between the Colonel (later General) and the Supreme Command very bad. The bad relationship lasted for the remaining part of the war and did not improve when Hansen later became Secretary of War.

At the beginning of May, General Hedemann moved his headquarters to Funen. During April the reserves had been called in and the army was built up to the strength of 20,000 men with eight new battalions. Though the new battalions were initially poorly equipped, the situation improved with time as new equipment came in. However everything was over-shadowed by the lack of experienced officers. The regular units could only release a few captains and lieutenants. It was therefore necessary to promote non-commissioned officers to the rank of lieutenants. Even dismissed non-commissioned officers were called in. Furthermore officers who had been out of active service for some years were re-drafted. Eventually 11 battalions, 19 squadrons of cavalry, 3 gun batteries and one battalion of volunteers were gathered on Funen. Three battalions were left on Zealand for protection of that island.

Whilst the Danish regrouped, on the Prussian side General Wrangel moved his army into Jutland. This was requested by the Parliament of the German Confederation as a counter action against the Danish naval blockade of the German Baltic and North Sea harbours. Wrangel moved north and took the fortress of Frederichia, which had been abandoned by the Danes. The skirmishers were positioned at Vejle but patrols moved as far north as Århus.

After the move into Jutland, General Wrangel demanded that the local populations supply his army with provisions. The burden of this was onerous and was only possible for a short time at each place; therefore the task of the patrols was to collect provisions, e.g., a force of two battalions and two squadrons reached the towns of Århus and Horsens where they succeeded, by taking the local prefect (*Stiftamtmand*) as hostage in collecting provisions at a value of 40,000 *Rigsbankdaler*.

After the initial collection of goods and after Wrangel had been ordered to leave Jutland he decided on 18 May to collect a special war tax as compensation for the losses which the German society had endured due to the naval blockade. The tax amounted to two million specie's (equivalent to four million *Rigsbankdaler*). Although the war tax was announced it was never collected.

Additionally the Schleswig Holstein army was ordered to collect 450 horses. The Danish local authorities resisted this but the Schleswig Holstein soldiers succeeded in collecting 346 horses.

Wrangel's push into Jutland was a sign to other governments that the war could have another purpose than just to liberate the Schleswig Holstein people from the Danish. After the battle at the town of Schleswig the Danish King asked the Swedish King Oskar I for military help. After consultation with his government King Oskar decided to send soldiers to Funen if the Germans moved into Jutland. When Wrangel made this move the Swedish government sent 15,000 troops to Southern Sweden with the intent that these could be transported to Denmark if necessary. A message was then sent to the Prussian Government in Berlin and to the Parliament in Frankfurt. Similarly the Russian Government was also submitting diplomatic notes. The British Government tried through a flurry of diplomatic activities to organise an armistice. The Prussian Government was alarmed over this new development and ordered General Wrangel to move south out of the Danish Kingdom and back into the Duchy of Schleswig. Wrangel was furious. He had asked for reinforcement but got nothing. On 25th May he ordered his troop to move south.

In the area from Rendsburg to Flensburg (a distance of some 50 km) General Wrangel had positioned 6,000–7,000 troops to cover the retreat and to guard against Danish attempts to land troops. In the Sundeved area two brigades were positioned with one at Gråsten as support, which amounted to 10,000 troops. The remaining part of the army was assembled in the area between Åbenrå and Vejle over a distance of some 50 km. The Schleswig Holstein army was used as vanguard and positioned at Vejle, one brigade was in Åbenrå to guard the headquarters, a brigade situated between Haderslev and Frederichia and another supported by a squadron was stationed at Tønder. The German army consisted of 28½ battalions, 23 squadrons and 74 field guns, in total 31,000 men. The army was scattered over a distance of 170 km.

The scatter made the conditions favourable for the Danish army and navy to concentrate troops giving local superiority. The Danish navy had full sovereignty of the sea and therefore the Danish Supreme Command was planning such a focused action.

However, the limitation of troop numbers able to be transported at any given time was a problem. A bridgehead was therefore necessary. Despite the army having withdrawn to the Island of Als, a bridgehead was preserved in the area opposite the town of Sønderborg. It was defended by some redoubts and connected to Als by a pontoon bridge which, if necessary, could be disconnected. The army could be transported from Funen to the village of Mommark on the eastern side of Als, where the Germans would not be able to observe the transport giving the Danes an advantage of surprise. The attack was planned to take place 28th May.

CHAPTER 3: 1848   69

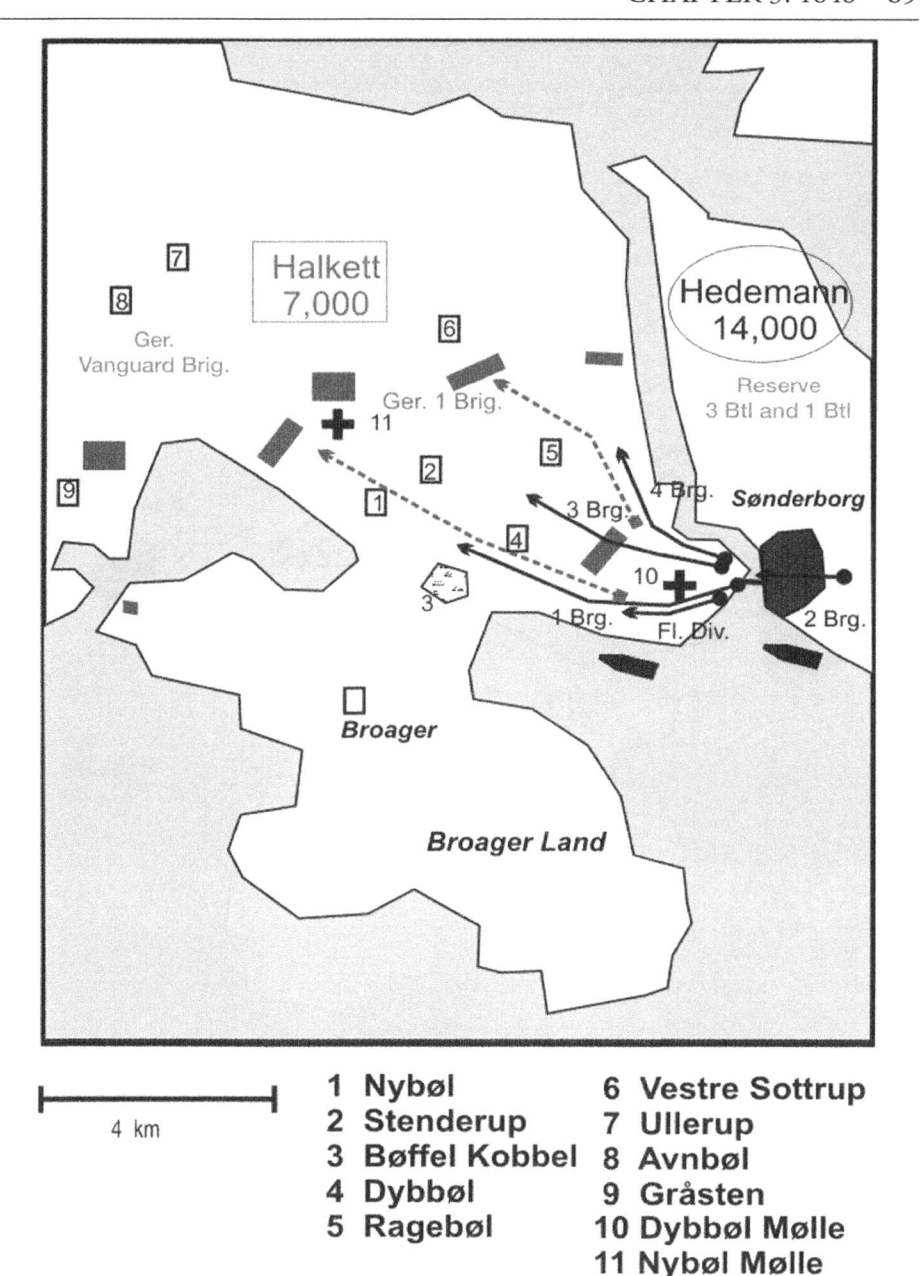

1 Nybøl	6 Vestre Sottrup
2 Stenderup	7 Ullerup
3 Bøffel Kobbel	8 Avnbøl
4 Dybbøl	9 Gråsten
5 Ragebøl	10 Dybbøl Mølle
	11 Nybøl Mølle

Map 9a Sundeved 28th May 1848 (1): 12:00–15:00 hours

70 FIRST SCHLESWIG HOLSTEIN WAR

1 Nybøl
2 Stenderup
3 Bøffel Kobbel
4 Dybbøl
5 Ragebøl
6 Vestre Sottrup
7 Ullerup
8 Avnbøl
9 Gråsten
10 Dybbøl Mølle
11 Nybøl Mølle

Map 9b Sundeved 28th May 1848 (2): 15:00–20:00 hours

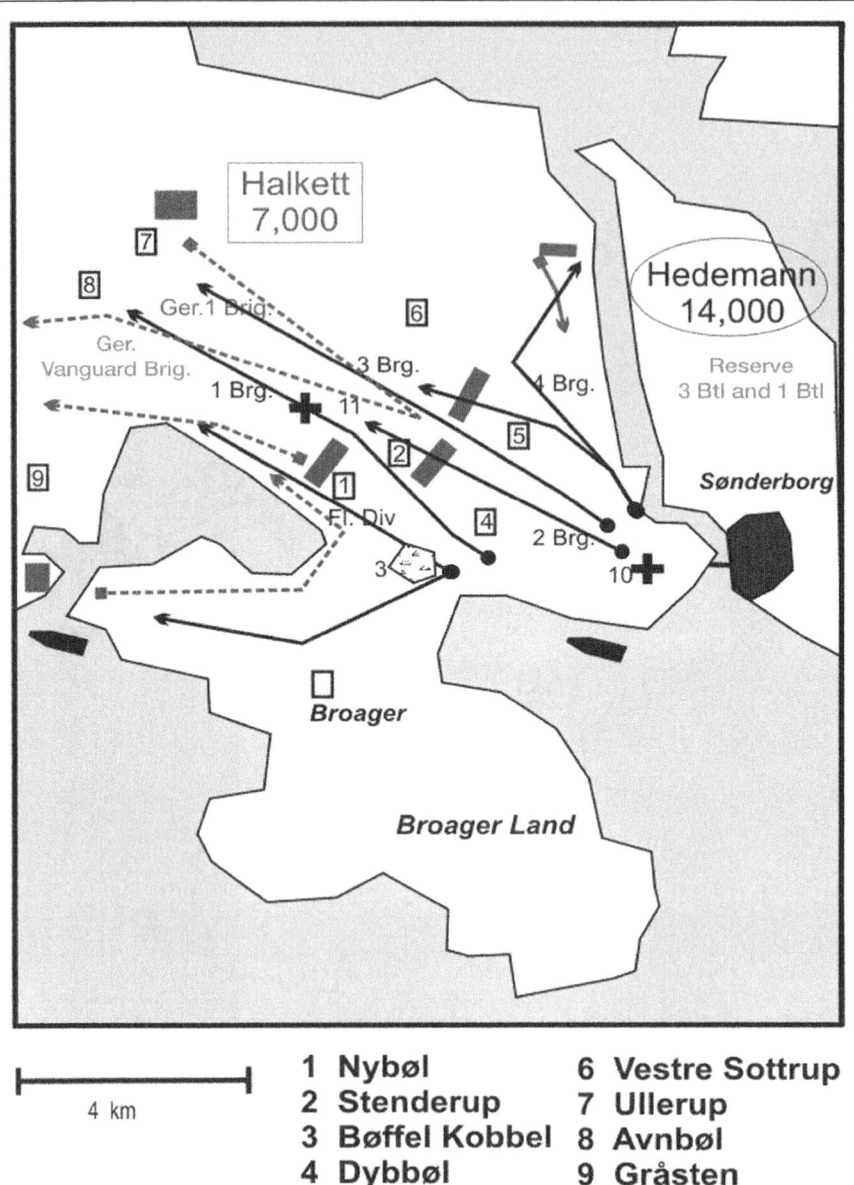

Figure 3.12 The Danish Army on Als attacks the Prussian army at Sundeved on 28th and 29th May 1848.

The CO of the German troops at Sundeved, General Halkett, had already realised the potential for such a surprise attack and therefore asked for reinforcements, but General Wrangel refused as he believed that the Danish force on Als was not large enough to present a significant threat.

The Danish continued the preparations. On 27th May the troops were transported to Als – partly to Mommark on the eastern side and partly to Høruphav. The latter area could be observed by the Germans so the landing took place after sunset.

The Danish Secretary of War Tscherning had initially approved General Hedemann's plan but when he heard about the retreat of the German troops he changed his mind. A military action could disturb the diplomatic activities. Therefore on 26th May he sent a messenger to General Hedemann requesting that Hedemann transfer the troops to Jutland and not to Als. The messenger did not reach General Hedemann on Funen, who was already on his way to the island of Als.

A message was sent through the optical telegraph (a row of flagpoles from one end of the island of Funen to the other where it was possible to send messages by signal flags) but the general did not react as the troops were already on Als. Eventually the messenger reached General Hedemann in Sønderborg on 28th May in the morning. The ensuing discussions resulted in a limitation of operations to a strong reconnaissance in order to force the skirmishers forward. General Hedemann and his staff did not want to demoralise the troops by a last minute cancellation.

While Wrangel had underestimated the Danish force on Als, the Danish Supreme Command had overestimated the German force in Sundeved. They had expected some 10,000 German troops.

At noon on 28th May in sunny weather, the Danish brigades finally marched over the bridge from Als to Sundeved. General Hansen (he had just been promoted) was CO for the entire force. The Flank Division, commanded by General Schleppegrell (he had also been promoted) was moved over the fjord by boats and thereafter operated on the left flank. The attack was directed towards Dybbøl mill, where the German skirmish line was situated. The 4th Brigade moved over the bridge as the last unit and thereafter took the road along the beach towards the north. The Flank Division was supported by a gun-barge, which was positioned in Vemminge fjord.

The German skirmishers at Dybbøl mill were in the process of being relieved. They consisted of one battalion, one platoon of mounted Hussars and two guns.

The Germans were not initially concerned by the Danish movements as they were used to daily alarms, when the Danish skirmishers moved out to protect the earthworks at the redoubts.

When they finally realised that this was serious a bonfire was ignited as a signal that the main attack by the Danish army had been initiated. Two battalions were moved forward to reinforce the skirmishers. At 14.00 hrs the Danish force was in the bridgehead and the German skirmishers on retreat. Despite further German reinforcement, the Danish army succeeded in forcing the German troops to retreat to Nybbøl Mill and Western Sottrup where the bulk of the German Sundeved force was positioned (figure 3.12).

General Halkett had been in Åbenrå for a conference with General Wrangel. At 13.00 hrs he began his journey back to his headquarters at Gråsten. Just as he was approaching headquarters he was informed about the ongoing battle. He rushed to Nybbøl where he arrived at 17.00 hrs. The bulk of his force was assembled there. In the middle of the German defence line immediately east of Nybbøl mill 16 guns were positioned. As soon as the Danish force reached Nybbøl mill the guns fired and were able to stop the attack. At that time (19.00 hrs) there were only six guns available to the Danish brigades and they soon took up the battle supported shortly after by two more guns. However the German guns were in a strong position and the Danish guns had to be pulled back.

The thunder from the guns could be heard far away and thus General Schleppegrell learned about the situation from where he was, at the central part of the front. By that time his brigade had taken the village Nybbøl. Continuing his attack he succeeded outflanking the German battalions at Nybbøl mill. Guns were moved forward and the German guns at Nybbøl mill were enfiladed from the south.

The cannonade caused some confusion among the German gunners and as the guns were closely spaced it was difficult to get them away. As soon as the German artillery fire stopped the brigades of General Hansen attacked again. With Schleppegrell's brigade endangering the positions at Nybbøl mill General Halkett decided to retreat towards Adsbøl and Gråsten.

At darkness, when fighting had ceased, the Danish skirmish line ran from Arnbøl to Rundkjær forest whereas the German troops were positioned at Adsbøl and Kværs. The Danes had suffered approximately 150 casualties, their opponents a similar number.

On the 28th, as soon as he heard about the battle, General Wrangel submitted a message to the brigade under General Bonin and to the Schleswig Holstein Brigade under the Prince of Nör, requesting that the troops march to Sundeved as soon as possible, and thereafter he rushed to Gråsten where he arrived on the 29th at 07.00 hrs. Bonin received the message at 02.00 hrs on the 29th and the brigade reached, by forced march, Årup just south of Åbenrå at 13.00 hrs.

The Schleswig Holstein troops were on the march west 20 km north of Tønder. General Wrangel decided that the Schleswig Holsteiners should instead be concentrated near Bov and so they returned and marched to Tinglev near Bov.

Bonin's brigade stayed near Kværs. It was of course essential for Wrangel to know where the Danish forces were so he ordered a vanguard of two battalions and one squadron accompanied by artillery to move forward. General Schnehen commanded the vanguard. They moved towards Nybbøl mill.

The Danish skirmishers withdrew towards Dybbøl, as they had no artillery. During the retreat the Danish artillery was moved forward and General Hansen ordered the retreat to stop.

The German troops were exhausted from the fighting which had taken place the day before and around 16.00 hrs General Halkett ordered the battalions to withdraw where after the Danish skirmish line was re-established.

The Danish losses were 140 dead and wounded and 11 prisoners of war whereas the Germans had 123 dead and wounded and 81 captured as prisoners of war.

Sundeved June 5th 1848

After the battle of 28 and 29 May General Wrangel decided to renew the attack on the Danish at Sundeved. The purpose was to force the Danish troops out of the bridgehead in order to remove the threat from his flank. Under the excuse of a parade for the birthday of the King of Hanover, two divisions of four brigades were assembled near Kværs. In parallel, reconnaissance operations were conducted towards Tønder and Åbenrå in order to protect against the Danish mounted brigade commanded by Colonel Juel who was situated near Haderslev and was supported by six battalions of infantry.

The German Division on the right flank was commanded by General Halkett and consisted of one Brunswick/Oldenburg/Mecklenburg Brigade with General Schnehen as CO and a Hanover Brigade with Colonel Marschalk as CO. In total 5,000 men in seven battalions, four squadrons and fourteen guns. The division on the German left flank was under the command of General Bonin and consisted of seven and a half battalions, two squadrons and 16 guns, in total 6,500 men, all Prussian. The remaining part of the army stayed in the area around Flensburg.

The plan was that General Halkett would advance from Gråsten at 10.00 hrs in two columns moving through Adsbøl and Nybbøl while Bonin's division as the left flank would advance in a longer and more northerly route. Because of the longer march for the northern division General Halkett delayed his departure by half an hour in order to reach the Danish skirmish line at the same time as Bonin and thereby coordinate the attack.

The Danish skirmish line was situated from Nybbøl fjord in the south via Korsmose mill and Snogebæk to Alssund in the north. The Danish Flank Division and part of the 4th Danish Brigade defended the line whereas the 3rd Danish Brigade was reserve at Dybbøl. The Danish General Schleppegrell had command. The remaining part of the army (the same as on 28 and 29 May) was on Als.

At noon the German right flank under Colonel Marschalk reached Nybbøl mill where they encountered the Danish skirmish line and the fighting commenced. The Danish skirmishers were forced to withdraw. At 13.00 hrs General Bonin's division on the left flank reached Sotrup but had to stop and rest for an hour due to the long march. At the same time the Danish troops on Als moved forward to reinforce the fighting units. General Bulow's 1st Brigade was the first unit to be at Dybbøl and by 16.00 hrs the entire Danish force was gathered at Dybbøl.

The German troops under General Schnehen had to slow down the attack in order to wait for General Bonin's division and when they finally reached Dybbøl, Colonel Marschalk's force attacked. However there was not room in the front for General Schnehen's men who had to stay back as reserve.

The German artillery also tried to take part in the attack. However on the eastern side of the front, it was enfiladed by both the Danish artillery and gun barges in Als fjord as well as distant guns positioned on Als, forcing it to withdraw.

At Dybbøl the German artillery had to be positioned in the open with no protection and was therefore an easy target for the Danish artillery as well as the gun barges in Vemmingebund fjord forcing a withdrawal there too.

At 17.00 hrs the situation was such that the German attack could not be supported by artillery, whereas the Danish could use their guns to full advantage.

General Wrangel then decided to end the attack and withdraw. A continuation would have required more troops, which were not available. The nearest reinforcement was the Schleswig Holstein Brigade at Flensburg. These were too far away to be of any use in the short term. When the Danish Supreme Command saw that the Germans were withdrawing they ordered all units to attack. In response the German troops had to retreat quickly and at darkness the Danish army had taken the terrain which had been lost earlier in the day.

Casualties were fairly even on both sides, circa 250 to 300 men each.

The period until the armistice

On 5th June Tscherning requested that the army stop further offensive actions due to the diplomatic negotiations which were taking place and that the mounted brigade in Jutland should be reinforced.

Coinciding with the battle at Sundeved, Danish Colonel Juel moved to Haderslev with his brigade only to be surprised by the Schleswig Holstein volunteer battalion under command of Major von der Tann. On 6th June von der Tann had reached Haderslev where his battalion attacked Colonel Juel's skirmish line. Colonel Juel believed that he had a large enemy force in front of him. He reacted by moving north without any reconnaissance and therefore never discovered how small the attacking unit actually was. This little victory was celebrated in Schleswig Holstein as a great one. When the Danish Supreme

Figure 3.13 **Cristoph von Krogh (1785–1860)** was from Haderslev in South Jutland. He joined the army at quite a young age and slowly advanced so that in 1848 he was major general. Secretary of War Tscherning had originally thought of Krogh as a potential commanding General. Due to his family ties to Schleswig and that his brothers had joined the Schleswig Holstein army he was not politically suited for the job. In 1849 he was given the command after General Hedemann, and again in 1850 at the battle at Isted. After the war Krogh was commanding general in Schleswig and later in Holstein and Lauenburg. In 1856 he had a stroke and retired from active service.

Command heard about the incident General Bülow was immediately dispatched with his brigade to Jutland where he took over the command from Colonel Juhl.

The Danish government had contacted the Swedish government with the view to obtain support for Denmark in the war. On 6th June, the King of Sweden and the King of Denmark with their governments met in Malmø in southern Sweden. The Swedes wanted an armistice and therefore requested that the Danes not embark on any offensive operations. They were prepared to support the Danes but not to send troops to Jutland as Wrangel had left the Kingdom and was back in the Duchy of Schleswig. On the other hand they were willing to send troops to Funen and in June some 5,000 men of the force which had been situated in Scandia, arrived on the island. They stayed until the armistice in August.

At the end of June General Wrangel moved north again. The Danish troops in Jutland, which had been reinforced, withdrew to Kolding. The activities of the armies slowly ceased as the Danes were forced by the Swedes to keep a low profile.

During May, peace negotiations took place between Prussia and Denmark in London with the British government acting as mediator, however the negotiations stopped because a proposal to divide the Duchy of Schleswig with one part to Denmark and another to Holstein was unacceptable to the Danish Government.

Figure 3.14 **Eduard von Bonin (1793–1865)** joined the army at a young age, so that in 1806 he participated in the battle at Jena and following that in various battles during 1813 to 1815. In 1850, after the campaign in Denmark, Bonin was back in Prussia and two years later was appointed Secretary of War. In 1854 during the Crimean War he had to resign as he had been supporting a pro-Russian policy. In 1858 he became secretary again under Prince Wilhelm, the later Emperor. However due to disagreement with the Prince he resigned a year later and then became commanding officer in Koblenz.

The British Prime Minister, Lord Palmerstone, therefore forwarded a revised proposal. Negotiations continued in Malmø where an armistice convention was finally agreed. All it needed was to be ratified by the Kings of the two countries.

Prussia however had got itself into an embarrassing situation. The Parliament in Frankfurt would not agree to the armistice. The Prussian King could therefore not ratify the armistice without getting into a controversial situation with the other countries of the German Confederation. The Danish King ratified and General Hedemann was instructed to sign the armistice papers.

General Wrangel on the other hand had been instructed not to sign and make the excuse that he was General for the Confederate army only. On 17 July a temporary armistice was signed while the officers negotiated the final agreement. These negotiations failed and so General Hedemann on 24th July declared the temporary armistice null and void.

On the same day, in Denmark, the Secretary of War, Tscherning, arrived at the headquarters of the Danish Army on Funen and took the opportunity to sack General Hedemann as Supreme Commander. General Krogh was to take over as Supreme Commander, Læssøe continued as Chief of Staff.

It is not clear why Tscherning sacked Hedemann but from correspondence between Læssøe and Tscherning it appears that Læssøe preferred Krogh as commander. Hedemann was very disappointed and surprised. Many officers supported Hedemann and sent supporting letters to the ministry. He was then sent to Copenhagen where he was in charge of a military commission until he retired in 1854. Five years later he died, totally blind.

Cristoph von Krogh (1785–1860) was from Haderslev in South Jutland (figure 3.13). He joined the army as a young man and was promoted slowly so that in 1848 he was a Major General. Secretary of War Tscherning had originally thought of Krogh as commanding general but due to his family ties to Schleswig and the fact that his brother had joined the Schleswig Holstein army he was not politically suited for the job. In 1848 he was given the command after General Hedemann and again 1850 at the battle at Isted. After the war Krogh was Commanding General in Schleswig and later in Holstein and Lauenburg. In 1856 he had a stroke and had to retire from active service.

Since the agreement with the Swedes stopped the Danish army from making any larger offensive operations, the Danes decided to expand the naval blockade to cover more of the Prussian Baltic harbours. This action as well as the more hostile attitudes of Sweden, Britain, France and Russia towards Prussia made the Prussian Government reconsider its position. With this pressure in place, they managed to get the Chancellor of the German Confederation to support an armistice.

The negotiations in Malmø were resumed and finally a seven month armistice was agreed and ratified on the 30th August. On 5th September the Confederate German troops withdrew from Schleswig. The Schleswig Holstein provisional government protested in vain. The Prince of Nör, who for some time had been in opposition to the Schleswig Holstein provisional government, was forced to resign as Supreme Command of the Schleswig Holstein Army. He also resigned from the Provisional Government and left Schleswig Holstein. From then on played no important political role.

General Eduard von Bonin (figure 3.14) took over as Supreme Commander of the German forces. Bonin (1793–1865) also joined the army as a young man and in 1806 he participated in the battle at Jena and then in various battles during the Napoleonic wars in 1813 to 1815. In 1842 he became Colonel. During 1848 he was promoted Brigadier. The same year he was appointed as Commander in Chief of the Schleswig Holstein Army. In 1850 he was back in Prussia and two years later was appointed Secretary of War. In 1854 during the Crimean War he had to resign as he had been in favour of a policy which supported Russia, this not being official Prussian policy. In 1858 he became secretary again under Prince Wilhelm, the later Emperor. However due to disagreement with the Prince he resigned a year later and then became Commanding Officer in Koblenz.

Naval operations in 1848

In March 1848 the secretary of the navy, Zahrtmann, ordered that the minor ships be made ready first so that the naval operations could commence as soon as possible. So on 26th March the ships *Hekla, Skirner, Gejser, Najaden* and *St. Thomas*, as well as some gun barges, left Copenhagen.

A transport task force was gathered at the Korsør harbour on the west coast of Zealand under the command of Captain Tegner to assist in the transport of the army. During the year six steamers were used. When the army had been transferred to Funen Captain Tegner moved to the town of Assens on the north coast of Funen near Little Belt where he could organize the army transport for the various army operations. A squadron under commander Paludan, consisting of *Gejser*, *Galathea*, *Najaden*, *St. Thomas*, *Merkur* and *Hekla* as well as 10 gun barges and six gun dinghies operated in the Baltic sea outside Schleswig. On 29th April the frigates *Havfruen*, *Thetis* and the corvette *Flora* were ready and sent to blockade the harbours at the mouth of the river Oder in Prussia. On the west coast of Jutland and Schleswig a squadron of mostly smaller vessels gathered to control the shallow sea and its island offshore Schleswig. On 1st May a squadron consisting of the frigates *Bellona*, *Gefion*, *Thetis* and *Havfruen* were sent to the North Sea to blockade the rivers Elbe, Weser and Jade. At the same time one more frigate was sent to the Baltic.

The armistice period from August 1848 to April 1849

The armistice convention required that the naval blockade should be stopped and that both parties withdraw their armies from the Duchy apart from 2,000 troops. The period of the armistice was seven months. The soldiers from the Duchy of Schleswig should be separated from the soldiers from Holstein and gathered in separate battalions and stationed in Schleswig. The rest of the Schleswig Holstein army would be gathered in Holstein. The prisoners of war would be exchanged – some 1100 Germans were exchanged for 900 Danish.

A government of five people would be formed with two representatives elected by the Danish King and two by the Prussian King while the last member, the chairman, would be elected by both kings. Both Prussia and Denmark would, additionally, send one commissioner each to Schleswig Holstein to ensure that the armistice convention was observed. Britain was asked to be guarantor. The prisoners of war were exchanged.

The government of five never came about. The Duchies were so agitated by the armistice agreement that the Danish members of the government of five had to hide in Hamburg when they were travelling to Schleswig to start working.

The Frankfurt Parliament also protested but eventually accepted the armistice convention, only for this to cause rioting in Frankfurt when it became public knowledge. Similar unrest occurred in other places in Germany.

As the Danish members of the government of five could not do their jobs, the Danish government elected two new members and on 22nd October they finally started work. The original provisional government resigned while the new one immediately ratified the laws of the previous provisionals including the new Schleswig Holstein constitution.

This was clearly in disagreement with the armistice convention and the Danish commissioners protested. In London, where new negotiations were ongoing, the British had proposed a division of the Duchy of Schleswig which was unacceptable to the Danes. The instruction to the Danish negotiator was that Schleswig should be separated from Holstein. If that was not possible a division with a line south of the one proposed by the British (from the town of Schleswig to

Husum in the west) was thought acceptable. King Frederik VII could however not agree to any division of his land and the Danish government therefore resigned.

After the armistice had been signed Frederik VII went to Als and Jutland to visit the army. He was saluted by the troops at large parades. At the parade in Jutland a new song was presented which ended with the following line 'This shall not happen'. When the king heard this he raised himself up and shouted 'This will not happen'. He then referred to the separation of Schleswig from Denmark. The officers were all cheering him. The King probably expressed the common opinion of the Danes, and thereby showed that a division of Schleswig was not political possible. The incident became known in Schleswig Holstein and was met with anger.

Both in Schleswig Holstein and in Denmark efforts were ongoing to create a new democratic constitution. The Danish constitution was eventually agreed and signed on 5th June 1849.

Chapter 4

1849

During the winter of 1848–1849 there was an attempt to reorganise the Danish army, with little success. Minor things were changed, such as the strength of a battalion was increased to 1,000 men. The supply and depot services were organised so that each battalion had its own supply company. The new Secretary of War, General Hansen, increased the army by three battalions so that in April 1849 there were 29 infantry battalions and 18 squadrons of cavalry, in total 41,000 troops and 6,000 horses. The artillery had eight cannon and two espignol batteries. General Krogh stayed as Supreme Commander with Lieutenant Colonel Læssøe as his chief of staff.

During the winter the Secretary of War, General Hansen, had discussed a new plan of operation for the spring campaign with General Krogh and his staff. Both the Chief of Staff and the Secretary of War had each prepared a strategy but they could not agree on which to use. In 1848 Tscherning had some plans to hire a French general as Supreme Commander which had not materialised.

However in the winter of 1849 this idea was revived and the French General Fabier was asked to come to Denmark as a consultant to the Secretary.

General Krogh went to Copenhagen and the negotiations between Krogh, the Secretary of War and the Secretary of the Navy were concluded with the approval of General Hansen's strategy, which was to land the bulk of the army at Eckernförde while a force of eight to ten thousand men moved south from Denmark. Furthermore the navy would sail into the fjord of Kiel and occupy the town with enough men to secure the operation which included the destruction of all 'enemy' military equipment including ships, guns and depots. If the locals resisted they should be treated with the outmost strictness.

It is worthwhile to note that this plan is void of any political repercussions as a result of the campaign. Fortunately it was never implemented as Kiel had been the place where the revolution had first commenced in 1848 and was so symbolic that it would have brought great enmity to the Danish from the Germans. It would have also given Prussia another excuse to send troops, and it is speculative as to how the Swedes would have reacted. There is only one short remark to be found on the forthcoming operation in the summaries of the Danish Cabinet meetings but with no reference to the political situation including a reaction from Sweden. It seems that a long-term strategy was missing.

General Fabier was thinking more long term as he recommended a more defensive attitude until other events forced the Prussian government to be distracted by other things, whereby the Danish army only had to deal with the Schleswig Holstein army. He furthermore recommended continuing the naval blockade.

The preparations for General Hansen's strategy commenced and the army was concentrated on Als and in Jutland. In early April the Secretary of War, General Hansen, together with General Fabier travelled to Als to participate in a conference where all the high ranking officers of the army and the navy were gathered. The Secretary of War also had a power of attorney from the Cabinet to commence fighting in case the German army moved over the river Eider.

The strategy of the Secretary of War was not well received by the officers of the staff and the secretary was forced to accept another plan prepared by Colonel Læssøe. This plan required that the army move out as far as possible on Sundeved while Dybbøl was fortified. The force in Jutland would stay and await the enemy actions. The navy should support the army's campaign by attacking the Schleswig Holstein strongpoints at Flensburg, Åbenrå and Eckernförde. The Secretary demanded though that the force in Jutland, which was commanded by General Rye, should move forward. It consisted of one infantry brigade and two mounted brigades. The rest of the army was on the island of Als.

General Bonin had not wasted his time during the winter months. He had reorganised the Schleswig Holstein army emulating the Prussian model. Compulsory service was introduced and he had hired a number of Prussian officers. At the outbreak of hostilities in 1849 the army consisted of 14 battalions each with 900 men, 10 squadrons and 46 pieces of artillery, in total 14,000 men and 3,500 horses. He had also formed a reserve brigade of five battalions and three squadrons from the younger and older generations. This brigade would be used as a guard protecting the flanks. The Schleswig Holstein army therefore had a total strength of 20,000 men.

The Prussian general, Karl Ludwig Ernst von Prittwitz (1790–1871) had been appointed as Supreme Command for the entire German force in Schleswig Holstein. Prittwitz (figure 4.1) joined the army at 13 (1803) as a standard bearer. After attending the Academy in 1812 he became staff officer and participated in the Napoleonic wars on the Prussian side. In 1830 he had been promoted to Colonel commanding the troops which crushed the rebellion in 1848 in Berlin. After the 1852 war he was given the command of the Prussian Guard division. The following year he withdrew from active service.

During the winter of 1848/1849 Prittwitz was instructed to keep his force concentrated with orders that the Danish army should be pursued and destroyed if possible. Though he was told to avoid moving his army from the Duchy of Schleswig into the Kingdom of Denmark, he was given leeway to cross the border if need be.

The entire German force counted 68 ¼ battalions, 40 squadrons of mounted units and 153 guns (including the Schleswig Holstein army) in total 61,000 men and 12,250 horses. At the end of March, 1849 Prittwitz moved into the Duchies. General Bonin had already pushed northwards with his vanguard stationed at Sundeved and his headquarters in Flensburg.

The interim government of the Duchies resigned on 26th March and was replaced by a new provisional government approved by the Frankfurt parliament. The members of the provisional government were Besler and Count Reventlow-Pretz. They could however, not agree on a third member, and the new provisional government therefore consisted of only those two.

Figure 4.1 **Karl Ludwig Ernst von Prittwitz (1790–1871)** joined the army in 1803 as standard bearer. After attending the officers' academy in 1812 he became staff officer. He participated in the Napoleonic wars as a Prussian officer. In 1830 he had advanced to colonel. He commanded the troops which crushed the rebellion in 1848 in Berlin. In 1849 he was given command of the German troops in Denmark, and after the war in 1852 he was given the command of the Prussian Guard Division. The following year he withdrew from active service.

Sundeved 1849

On 2nd April in the evening the Armistice ended. The Danish army had occupied the bridgehead opposite Sønderborg and on 3rd April in the morning the army moved over the bridge into Sundeved. During the same day Gråsten was reached, though with minor encounters with the Schleswig Holstein skirmish line. The navy reconnoitred the sea outside Egernsund and Åbenrå and in both places the ships exchanged cannonades with onshore Schleswig Holstein gun batteries forcing them to retreat.

At Åbenrå the navy landed troops and occupied the town. The plan of the Danish Supreme Command was that the army should defend the occupied terrain. However, the Secretary of War, General Hansen, was in Sønderborg (he was actually laying in bed ill) and he demanded that the army should not progress any further. Instead redoubts and entrenchment should be constructed at Dybbøl. It was therefore decided to have the skirmish line move from Adsbøl via Ulderup to Als fjord. General Rye and his troops in Northern Schleswig moved south towards Haderslev, but on 4th April he was ordered to stop his advance due to changes in the operation at Sundeved.

The interference of the Secretary of War is surprising in view of his earlier very offensive strategy and can only be understood in the light of the more defensive recommendations of the French General Fabier. This may be confirmed by the summaries of the Cabinet meeting of 11th April 1849, where the Secretary of War informs the rest of the Cabinet about General Fabier's proposed defensive strategy. In any event the change of plans was not well received by the Danish Supreme Command.

General Prittwitz relieved the Schleswig Holstein army at Sundeved by calling in the 1st Division of the Confederate army. On 6th April the Hanoverian battalions moved forward towards Avnbøl where they met the Danish 1st Brigade. The fighting lasted the whole afternoon but in the evening the German battalions had to retreat and the Danish army took up the positions it had occupied in the morning.

The navy operations and the affair at Eckernförde

In 1849 the Royal Danish Navy fielded more ships than the previous year. In the North Sea, apart from the small ships in the shallow water around the islands of the west coast, the squadron consisted of four frigates, one corvette and a steamer. The Baltic squadron consisted of one ship of the line, four brigs, two smaller sailing vessels, five steamships and 18 gun barges. In addition to this there were a large number of transport vessels.

As mentioned earlier the plan of the Danish Supreme Command was that the navy should participate in an action towards Eckerneförde simultaneously with the army operations. This operation was given to F. A. Paludan, the commander of the ship of the line *Christian VIII* supported by the steamer *Hekla*, the frigate *Gefion*, the steamer *Gejser* and three cutters. The latter transported a company of the 11th Battalion.

The ship of the line carried 84 guns, the frigate 48 guns and the steamers each eight guns. The idea was to disturb the enemy as much as possible and, if feasible, land troops to destroy the onshore gun batteries. This objective was prepared by the Supreme Command and was forwarded by the Chief of the Baltic naval squadron to Commander Paludan. The ship of the line had only been in the sea for two weeks with a totally new crew. Due to rough weather it had not been possible to carry out any gunnery exercises. It had been possible to have the crew training at battle stations just once, and fire one salute with all the guns just to become familiarised with the sound.

The Commander was given the authority to go into battle, though he was not obliged to. However the order not to expose the steamers to enemy fire was quite clear. The ships departed from Als on 4th April and the same afternoon they reached Eckernförde fjord. At 18.00 hrs the ships entered the fjord together and anchored outside the reach of the Schleswig Holstein guns. The wind was blowing in an easterly direction.

The area was protected by the 3rd Reserve Brigade commanded by Captain Irminger and a reserve brigade of the German Federation commanded by the Duke of Sachen-Coburg-Gotha.

The Schleswig Holstein army had prepared two gun batteries protected by fortifications at the beach, one north and one south of the town. The northern one had six guns whereas the southern one had four guns. Both batteries had ovens in which the balls for the guns could be heated.

84 FIRST SCHLESWIG HOLSTEIN WAR

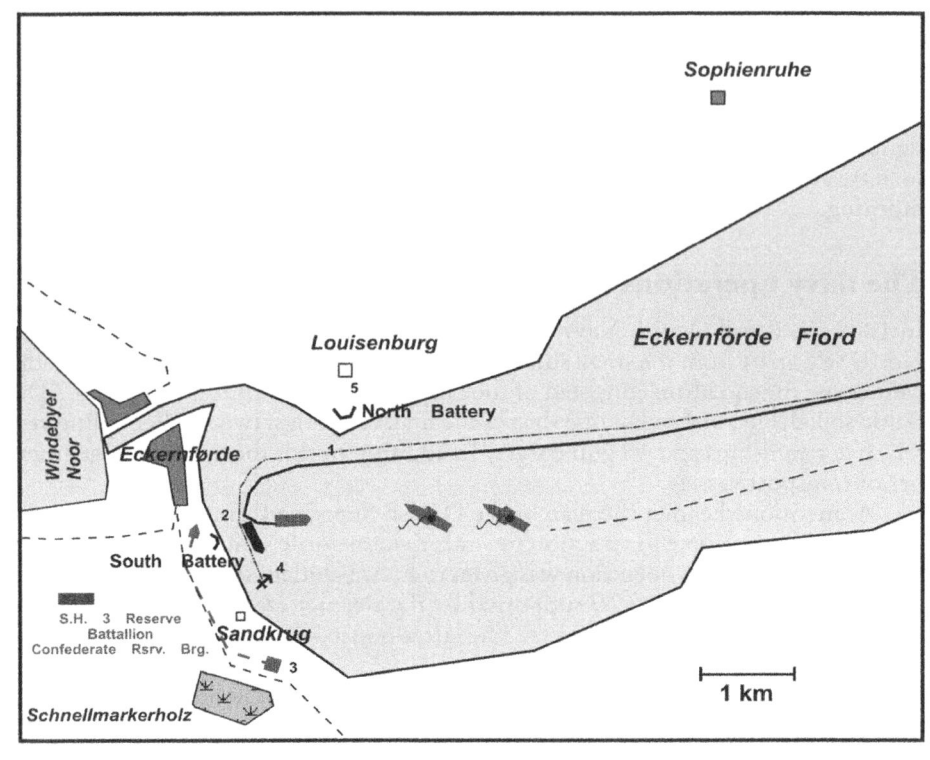

1 The ship of the line and the frigate makes several broadsides towards the north battery at 8.00 hrs
2 The ship of the line and the frigate initiates the fighting with the south battery at 8.15 hrs in the morning
3 The field battery moves from Sandkrug to Eckernförde during the cease-fire
4 The ship of the line grounds at 18.00 hrs
5 The position of the other part of the field battery

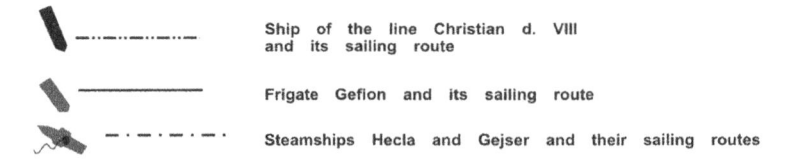

Ship of the line Christian d. VIII and its sailing route

Frigate Gefion and its sailing route

Steamships Hecla and Gejser and their sailing routes

Map 10 Eckernförde 5th April 1849

When the Danish ships entered the fjord, the Schleswig Holstein Reserve Brigade was notified and two battalions and some guns were sent to Eckernförde. The field guns were positioned on the hills above the northern ramparts and at Sandkrug (map 10).

On 5th April in the morning the commanding officers of the Danish ships assembled on the ship of the line with Commander Paludan. During this conference he decided to carry out the action despite the prevailing easterly wind, which had calmed down. The other officers concurred. Paludan clearly had no expectation of making a surprise attack so he decided to abandon the landing operation with his troops.

At 07.00 hrs the ships, apart from the cutters, sailed into the fjord, the ship of the line and the frigate stayed on the northern side so that they sailed towards the northern battery and could therefore give it several broadsides. The guns of the ships were fired in one volley. One of the 24 pound guns onshore was damaged and the flagpole knocked down. Thereafter the ships turned towards the southern battery and gave that a broadside as well. The ships anchored 400 to 500 m from land and continued the enfilade of the southern battery. The distance to the northern battery was 1,200 m and only the astern guns could be used to shoot at this target. The northern battery had only two 84 pound guns that could reach the ships.

Shortly after arrival the frigate was turned by the wind so that it had its stern towards the south battery. It was therefore only possible to use the astern guns and two of them were damaged by enemy fire. The steamship *Gejser* was called in to try to tow the frigate back to the old position but the cable broke and it was not accomplished at the first attempt. In the second attempt the ship was turned slightly. In the meantime the enemy guns had shot at the ship and damaged it, causing many casualties. The two steamers took position in the fjord and commenced shooting at the onshore batteries. The steamer *Hekla* was hit and damaged.

The ship of line continued its bombardment and suffered only a little damage. Paludan then decided to stop the fighting partly because of the poor condition of the frigate and partly because the field batteries were actively taking part in the shooting. He expected that there would be reinforcements for the Schleswig Holstein gun crews. Around 10.00 hrs the steamer *Hekla* was called in to try and tow the frigate out. Unfortunately *Hekla* damaged its rudder and had to retreat. The south battery continued to concentrate its fire on the frigate. The Commanding Officer therefore informed Paludan that the situation was critical, the boat was so damaged that it could not move by its own sail and had so many casualties that it could not maintain the fire towards the enemy. Therefore the steamer *Gefion* came in to try to tow the frigate. When the cable was in position the steamer was hit in the engine. It had to cut the cable and pull the anchor. Paludan therefore gave the steamer the order to retreat, which it did with half engine power. The next attempt was to warp the frigate out with the help of the crew from the ship of line and its barge. Slowly it was pulled out but due to the increase in the easterly wind it was difficult. On the frigate the rig was damaged and it had to be repaired to prevent it falling down. The southern battery had not yet been silenced.

Paludan now tried a desperate ploy. He sent a negotiator ashore with a proposal to cease fire so that the ships could leave. If the Schleswig Holstein army did not agree he would start firing at the town of Eckernförde. When the Danish negotiator reached the shore, the Schleswig Holstein batteries ceased fire. He was told that he would get an answer within half an hour.

The cease-fire was very convenient for the Schleswig Holstein crews, for the guns of the north battery were out of use and needed repairing. Only two guns of the south battery were usable, although they were so overheated that they would have had to cease fire anyway. Furthermore there was a shortage of ammunition.

The field battery was situated too far away at Sandkrug to be able to reach the ships. The Schleswig Holstein crews used the cease-fire optimally and new ammunition was brought forward. The damaged guns were repaired and in both batteries the crew started to heat the cannon balls in preparation for new firing. The field battery was moved so that it was within reach of the ships and could enfilade them from the astern. The message from the Commander made it clear to the Schleswig Holstein officers that the ships were in trouble. On the frigate the warping continued but due to increasing easterly wind the progress was slow.

The ship of line was intact with only limited damage and Paludan wanted to stay and support the frigate. In the meantime the damage on the steamer *Hekla* was repaired so that it could navigate. It therefore moved in to tow the frigate but the north battery then commenced firing at it. It was now 16.00 hrs. The captain of the steamer did not feel it was safe to continue the operation and therefore left the fjord and went back to Sønderborg. The steamer *Gejser* was of no help as the damage could only be repaired in the harbour and it was therefore also ordered home.

At 16.30 hrs Paludan received his answer; the Schleswig Holstein crew had no intention of maintaining the cease-fire. The threats of firing at the town were dismissed and it was made clear that it was the Commander's responsibility if he carried out his threats. At 17.00 hrs the firing started again. The frigate could not be saved and the Captain on the ship decided, together with his officers, to surrender. This decision was conveyed to Paludan about 17.45 hrs and the flag of the frigate was pulled down. The batteries on land continued shooting until an officer was sent ashore to inform them about the surrender.

The ship of line was also enfiladed by the field battery which used heated balls and grapeshot. The ship returned fire and also threw a few shots at the town. Paludan now decided to retreat and at 17.30 hrs he ordered the anchor to be pulled. Even before this was achieved the grapeshot damaged the sails. Though the ship got wind in its sails it was not enough to enable it to use its rudder and it drifted ashore and grounded. The heated balls had started a fire onboard and Paludan therefore decided to surrender. The crew started to extinguish the fire and throw the powder into the sea.

The commanding officer for the south battery came onboard and demanded that Paludan come ashore and surrender. Similarly the crew should stop the fire fighting and hasten onshore otherwise the shooting would continue. Shortly after, flames came out of the hatches and gun ports and before the Schleswig Holstein commanding officer disembarked at 20.30 hrs the ship exploded (figure 4.2).

Figure 4.2 The Eckernförde affair - the ship of the line *Christian VIII* explodes. In the foreground is the Schleswig Holstein redoubt with facilities for heating the iron balls for the guns.

The remaining crew, mostly wounded, doctors, and orderlies as well as the Schleswig Holstein CO, were killed. The Danish casualties during this battle were 106 dead and 958 prisoners while the Schleswig Holstein army suffered 22 dead and wounded.

This victory was celebrated in Germany and Schleswig Holstein. To the Danes, who regarded themselves as a seafaring nation, the episode was an embarrassment. When Paludan returned to Denmark later in the year after the exchange of prisoners during the winter cease-fire, he together with the Chief of the Baltic naval squadron were court-martialled and sentenced to prison. Both officers felt that they had become scapegoats for bad judgements by the Supreme Command.

After the battle, the frigate *Gefion* was repaired and brought into the navy of the German Confederation under the name *Eckernförde* and later into the Imperial navy under the name *Gefion* until it was scrapped in 1891.

The affair at Eckernförde was used by the Secretary of War General Hansen to remove General Krogh and his Chief of Staff Captain Læssøe from their commands and instead make General Bülow the Supreme Commander with Colonel Flensburg as his Chief of Staff.

Frederik Rubeck Henrik Bülow (1791–1858) was born in South Jutland (figure 4.3). He was from a family who had immigrated to Denmark from Mecklenburg during the 1600s. The family had been officers or diplomats serving the Danish King. F. Bülow joined the army in 1805 in Rendsburg and had been promoted to lieutenant in 1809. He participated in various fighting during the Napoleonic Wars. He preferred the service in the army from the service at the court which some of his family members could have organised for him. In 1847 he had advanced to Colonel. He offered his service as Supreme General to Tscherning in

Figure 4.3 **Frederik Rubeck Henrik Bülow (1791–1858)** was born in South Jutland. He was from an old Mecklenburg family, who had emigrated to Denmark in the 1600s. The family had been officers or diplomats serving the Danish King. F. Bülow joined the army in 1805 in Rendsburg and had advanced to lieutenant in 1809. He participated in various fighting during the Napoleonic wars. He was promoted to lieutenant general after the battle at Fredericia and was given a donation of 20,000 Rigbanksdaler. However his bad health prevented him from taking command the following year. When he recovered he became a general in Schleswig and three years later in Copenhagen. In 1856 he retired from the army and lived in South Jutland on his estate until his death in 1858.

1848 but the offer was refused. His excellent performance in the battles at Bov and Schleswig made Tscherning promote him to Major General.

North Jutland until Fredericia

The Schleswig Holstein army had originally been at Sundeved but had been relieved by the Prussians. Now their army moved north and soon its vanguard units met the Danish skirmishers from General Rye's Brigade situated at Kolding. The new Supreme Commander General Bülow therefore decided to reinforce the army in Jutland.

General Bonin, the commander of the Schleswig Holstein army, had meanwhile decided to push northwards despite direct orders from General Prittwitz not to enter the Kingdom. General Bonin had 14 battalions, 10 squadrons and 46 guns under his command.

1 It should be recalled that the border between the Duchy of Schleswig and the Kingdom of Denmark at that time was situated at Kolding.

The Danish Supreme Command concentrated three brigades (15 battalions, 16 squadrons and 46 guns) north of Kolding and on 23rd April they attacked the Schleswig Holstein army with the intention that General Rye's Brigade would try to surround it. However, the mission was not successful and at noon General Bülow ordered the army to retreat (map 11).

The Schleswig Holstein army considered this as a victory and General Prittwitz therefore had to congratulate General Bonin, but at the same token told General Bonin that he had not been authorised to move that far north. In fact Prittwitz was so angry that in his reports to his superior in the Prussian Ministry of War he mentioned that he was prepared to relieve Bonin of his command next time he exceeded his orders.

Prittwitz was dealing with conflicting orders; the Confederate Government wanted him to move into the Kingdom but the Prussian Ministry of War did not. Furthermore Prittwitz was critisized in the German newspapers for lack of action. Prittwitz then threatened the Prussian Ministry with his resignation if he was not allowed to obey the Confederate Government. The Schleswig Holstein Provisional Government was dissatisfied with the situation as well and in a meeting with the General tried to convince him to continue the move north no later than 5th May.

By the 5th Prittwitz had not heard anything from the Prussian Government so on 6th May he gave the order to move north. He then transferred his headquarters north to Kolding where he finally received the order from Prussia that he was allowed to obey the Confederate Government.

On 7th May the two armies clashed again, first at Viuf just north of Kolding and at Gudsø east of Kolding. The battle was not successful for the Danish army and General Bülow ordered the majority to retreat to Fredericia whereas General Rye's Brigade moved north again.

The Schleswig Holstein Army followed the Danes to Fredericia and surrounded them. The Prussian army with the other German units under General Prittwitz followed General Rye as he headed north.

With his entry into the Kingdom, General Prittwitz was in enemy and unwelcoming territory. Although the northern part of the Duchy of Schleswig was Danish, Prittwitz was commanding an army which at least formally was fighting for the Schleswig Holstein population. However in the Kingdom he had no support. In order to get supplies for his army he had to make requisitions from the Jutland population. The local authorities (*Amtmand*) were asked to organise the supplies. This did not go smoothly and every now and then the German soldiers had to put pressure on the locals.

One of the most obstinate *Amtmand* was arrested and sent to Rendsburg though he was released soon after. Irrespective of the threats the supplies came in slowly and ran out quickly and so, the German army could not stay for long periods in the same place. General Prittwitz therefore had to move north at regular time intervals in order to get fresh supplies. Requisition commands were also sent to western Jutland.

General Rye (figure 4.4) told local officials in the counties only to obey if the Prussians were threatening the use of force. He also sent a couple of squadrons and a company of infantry to west Jutland to disturb the German requisition and even succeeded in capturing some of the companies undertaking the operation. The

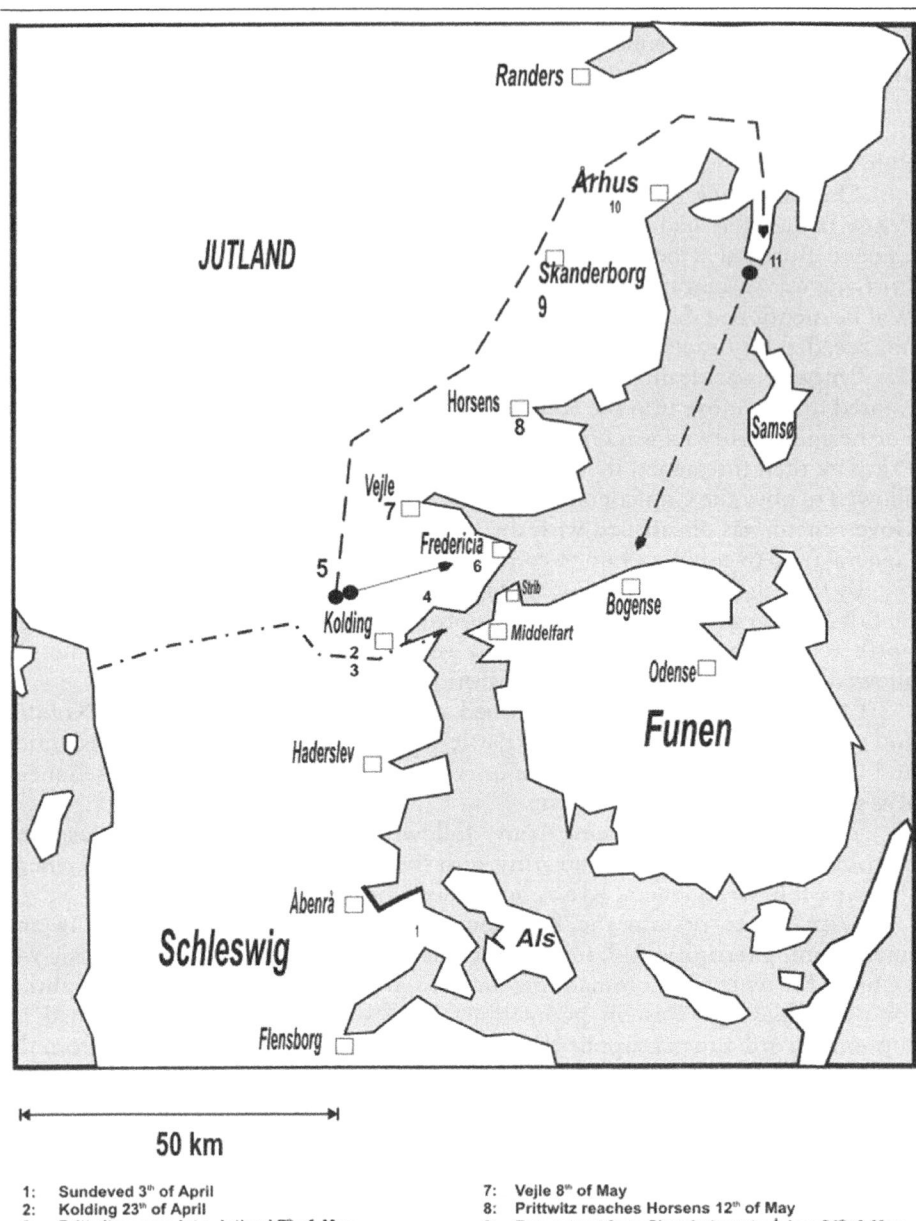

90 FIRST SCHLESWIG HOLSTEIN WAR

Map 11 General Rye's retreat in 1849

Figure 4.4 **Olaf Rye (1791–1849)** was born in Norway from a family who traditionally served the Danish King. Painting made in 1861 by P.Meidelt with permission from the family of General Rye.

Germans were therefore forced to strengthen the commands and in June two battalions were sent westwards.

While the German army pushed northward experiencing minor skirmishing with General Rye's brigade, Rye organised an intelligence service. The chairmen of the parish councils were informed of every move of the German troops in their parishes. This information was brought to the Supreme Command of the Danish army by a chain of dispatch riders. General Rye therefore always knew where the German army was positioned but the opposite was not always the case.

In the middle of May, General Prittwitz had moved to a position south of the town of Skanderborg. The political situation in Germany was such that he did not want to press further north but once more the supply situation forced him to push forward. On 24th May his vanguard moved north to find that General Rye and his brigade had disappeared. It took several days before they finally located them at Århus.

General Rye had received orders to withdraw north to Helgenæs on the peninsula of Mols. General Prittwitz pressed ahead towards Århus and on the 31st May skirmishing forced Rye out of the town. It was during these skirmishes that one of the few encounters of the war between cavalry units took place.

During June there was not much activity.

The situation was now that the German forces were once more scattered. At Sundeved and Åbenrå there were 9,000 troops positioned at each place; at Flensburg a brigade of 4,000 men; at Fredericia the Schleswig Holstein army had 14,000 troops, and at Århus and Skanderborg, Prittwitz had 18,000 men.

The Danes were scattered too but could at any time transport 7,000 men over the sea. General de Meza was on Als with 15,000 men, General Bülow on Funen with 8,000 men and Rye at Helgenæs and Århus with 9,000 men. Fredericia had its garrison of 4,000 men.

The Schleswig Holstein army at Fredericia was in fact isolated, as it would take a day to bring the nearest reinforcement. At the end of June General Rye and his Danish Brigade marched north and on 29th June, four battalions with a battery of guns were shipped from Helgenæs to Bogense on Funen.

At this time the Prussian Government asked General Prittwitz to request an armistice, but the Danes refused.

Fredericia

The fortress of Fredericia was built by the Danish King Frederik III in 1650 but before it was finished, war broke out with Sweden and by 1657 Frederiksodde, as it was called at that time, was captured by the Swedish army. During the Great Northern War from 1709 to 1710 the fortress was renovated, though from that point in time it was not maintained.

Fredericia is a typical fortified city with wide straight streets running at right angles to each other. The fortifications are 1,800 m long and in plan view it is the shape of an arch, which faces towards the west and north. It has 11 bastions and a flooded moat in front (map 12).

The fortress is situated on a small peninsula so that the eastern and southern sides face the sea. At the tip of the peninsula the last stronghold, the Citadelle, was built. In 1848 the fortress was in such a bad condition that it was abandoned by the Danish army and the Schleswig Holsteiners occupied it but then abandoned it and returned to Schleswig Holstein during the Armistice.

When the Danes returned to the fortress they began to repair it, with Colonel Lunding in charge. In February 1849, using a large contingent of troops he succeeded in having most of the necessary repair work finished in preparation for when the Schleswig Holstein army would arrive at the gates to begin their siege. In this way the parapet, the places for the cannons and the gates to the fortress were repaired. The dams in front of the gates were replaced by bridges, which could easily be removed.

The moats were once again filled with water. Furthermore with the construction of a dam at the mouth of the small stream west of the fortress, the low-lying areas called 'the Mill pasture' and 'Ullerupå valley' were flooded. A small redoubt was constructed at the southern end of the dam in order to prevent enemy infiltration. Finally smaller gates were built in the fortifications with protected areas in front to be used for sorties by the garrison.

The 'Citadelle', which had been damaged in 1848 by the bombardment of the Danish army using guns positioned on Funen, was repaired. It was the least exposed part of Fredericia and was therefore prepared as storage and shelter. In order to improve the sea connections to the fortress two landing piers were constructed outside the 'Citadelle', these are the so-called eastern and southern piers. Nine of the bastions were armed with 100 cannons of various calibres.

CHAPTER 4: 1849   93

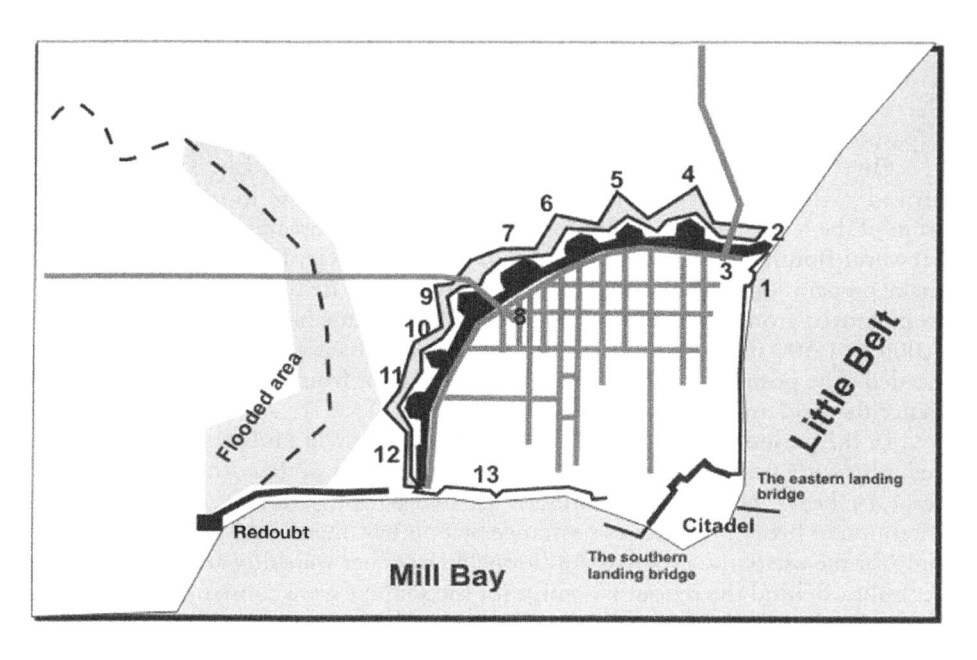

Map 12 Fredericia

1 Norway Bastion
2 Denmark Bastion
3 Kings gate
4 Kings Bastion
5 Queens Bastion
6 Prins Christians Bastion
7 Prins Georg's Bastion
8 Prins Gate
9 Prinses Bastion
10 Slesvig Bastion
11 Holsten Bastion
12 Oldenborg Bastion
13 Delmenhorst Bastion

It was planned, as the siege progressed, that the smaller cannons would be replaced with heavier ones. To support the fortress a number of redoubts with heavy artillery were constructed on the other side of Little Belt on Funen. These were especially designed to enfilade the flooded area at 'Mill Pasture', which Colonel Lunding considered to be the most exposed part of the fortress. The garrison consisted of 6,000 men of which 1,000 on a daily basis were rotated from the reserve on Funen. The artillery was manned by 700 gunners who were not used as part of the rotation in order to keep a staff of experienced gunners in the fortress.

On 7th May, the Schleswig Holstein army commanded by General Bonin arrived at the gates of Fredericia. Bonin's instructions were to secure the area in front of the fortress and prevent the Danish army from breaking out of Fredericia. However Bonin had his own agenda – to take Fredericia. He ordered his army to make preparations to build redoubts for batteries and he ordered heavy siege guns to be moved from Rendsburg to Fredericia. Field guns had a maximum range of 1,000 to 1,500 m but poor accuracy. For greater precision, half the distance was needed. The position of the Schleswig Holstein guns from Fredericia was 1,000 m hence the field artillery were useless as siege guns.

In the period 8th through 15th May, the Schleswig Holstein Army built six redoubts with artillery constructed west and north-west of the fortress (map 13). In total 14 heavy guns were positioned in five of the redoubts. It was Bonin's intention to break Fredericia's resistance by bombardment. The sixth redoubt was only for the use of the infantry. Additionally, trenches were dug around two of the redoubts. Behind the redoubts, camps for the soldiers were constructed e.g., at the Egum road and at Heise Inn. At the latter place the main supply camp was positioned.

Danish Colonel Lunding, in order to reconnoitre the Germans before they had constructed all the redoubts, ordered his garrison to carry out a minor sortie on 13th May with three battalions together with the cavalry units, which had remained in the fortress. The sortie did not reveal a lot on the Schleswig Holstein positions but at least Colonel Lunding got the impressions that the redoubts were mostly of a defensive nature.

On 16th May, the siege guns were in place and the Schleswig Holstein army began the bombardment of Fredericia. In three days over 1,000 shots were fired at the fortress causing some damage. The garrison replied with only about 300 rounds as it was not possible to hit the relatively small redoubts. It soon became clear to General Bonin that a simple bombardment was not enough to force the fortress to surrender and he had to consider other measures. He decided to cut the supply routes and ordered his units to attack the Danish redoubt at the flooded area. This was accomplished on 22nd May and the redoubt was taken. The Danish counterattack the same night was unsuccessful due to the fact that the Danish soldiers did not obey their officers in the first attack and retreated. The officers then managed to convince the soldiers to make two more attacks during the night but the redoubt was not retaken.

Bonin ordered three gun batteries placed at the coast of 'Mill Bay' in order to be able to enfilade the landing piers both at Fredericia and on the other side on Funen and thereby prevent supply to the fortress. The guns would also be used to keep the Danish gun barges at a distance. General Bonin had plans for more

CHAPTER 4: 1849 95

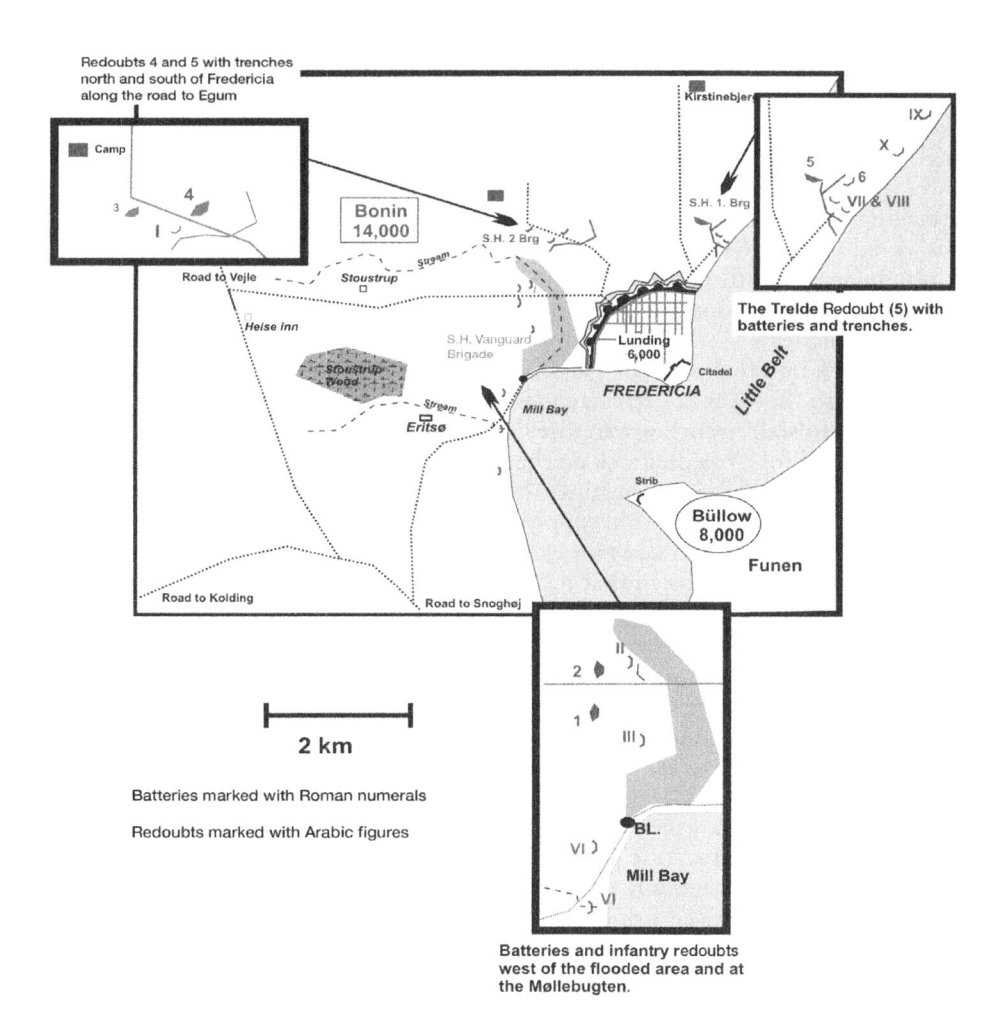

Map 13 Fredericia from 7th May to 6th July 1849

redoubts. On 3rd June the Schleswig Holstein army initiated another bombardment of Fredericia which lasted for five hours. The garrison answered back with a similar heavy bombardment. The purpose of this artillery duel was to cause confusion and damage inside the fortress in order to distract the attention from the real purpose – construction of another redoubt closer to the fortress from where it would be possible to hit targets within Fredericia.

When the bombardment ceased in the evening some 3,000 Schleswig-Holstein men moved out after darkness, of which 2,000 was a workforce used for the building of the redoubts. The remaining 1,000 men were assigned to force the Danish skirmish line back. The Danish skirmishers pulled back from the attacking soldiers but were soon reinforced. The fighting lasted for several hours. However, while the fighting and troop movements were occurring, the Schleswig Holstein artillery officer found that the area was too swampy for heavy siege guns and decided to abandon the constructions of the redoubts and instead extend the existing trenches.

Colonel Lunding did not know the Danish Supreme Command's plan for Fredericia so he sent a letter requesting information. He believed that the Schleswig Holstein trenches were the first part of a series of parallel trenches that would be used for a major attack on the fortress. Also, that the Schleswig Holstein army had succeeded in damaging the southern pier and he was afraid that Fredericia could be cut off from supply and therefore would have to be abandoned without any fighting. His concern would turn out to be too pessimistic.

After it had been shown that it was impossible to get the siege guns closer to the fortress, another heavy bombardment of Fredericia and the redoubts on the other side of Little Belt at Strib was initiated in order to cut the supply route.

During the next two weeks the guns on both sides thundered both day and night. In particular, the Schleswig Holstein guns at Mill Bay and Eritsø, which were perilous for the integrity of the fortress for they could reach Strib and the southern pier in Fredericia. The guns at the Egum road could only reach the town inside the fortress.

The Danish guns, especially those on the Holstein bastion, responded with a bombardment to destroy the guns at Mill Bay. Occasionally there was silence in order to fix any damage but every night the Schleswig Holstein gunners made repairs and recommenced firing the next day.

The Danish gunners learned to aim at the Schleswig Holstein batteries during daylight and then use this same trajectory at night. Fredericia did not capitulate despite the onslaught. The eastern pier was never damaged and the supply line never cut.

General Bonin therefore considered making redoubts north of the fortress. This would leave his army stretched over a long front; a dangerous position to be in if the Danes decided to make a sortie with a large force. But Bonin figured that if the Danes concentrated large forces in Fredericia he would be able to observe this and be warned in due time so he decided to go ahead with the construction of the northern redoubts. They could then be abandoned or reinforced. The retreat route for the northern units at Rands fjord to the north was reconnoitred and secured with a guard.

On 19th June the Schleswig Holstein units began construction of a camp at Kirstinebjerg north of Fredericia. The 1st Schleswig Holstein Brigade was moved there the following week and on 27th June the work on the redoubt began. This was constructed 600 m from the coast and supported by a system of trenches which ran from the coast to the redoubt. Behind the trenches the foundations for two gun batteries (nos. VII and VIII) were built, which would be able to enfilade the eastern pier. 500 m behind those, two more gun batteries were erected (nos. IX and X). These in particular were supposed to keep the Danish gun barges away.

The work proceeded slowly due to rainy weather. During this period General Bonin received a report that large amounts of Danish troops had been shipped out from Als. He could also see that a larger number of ships at Bogense had left, making it quite clear that the Danish army was in the process of concentrating troops somewhere. Bonin thought that it might be Fredericia so the construction work on the redoubt was therefore stepped up.

Inside Fredericia the work on the fortress continued during June at the same time as the artillery duels took place. The patrols which were sent out observed nothing special. However on 19th June the patrolling gun barges observed Bonin's construction work at Kirstinebjerg.

When the earthwork on the redoubt commenced on 27th June it was obvious that there was something special going on in the Schleswig Holstein lines. The batteries at Kirstinebjerg were a significant threat to the supply line and Colonel Lunding immediately ordered some of the heavy artillery to the northern bastions. When he also observed the construction of foundations for gun batteries on 30th June he gave the order for a sortie from Fredericia the same afternoon.

Six companies from various battalions, some cavalry units and a larger workforce were included in the task force. At around 15.00 hrs they moved out of the King's Gate. The attack came as a surprise for the Schleswig Holstein units. Their skirmishers pulled back and with a quick blow the Danes succeeded in taking the redoubt and trenches. The Schleswig Holstein units retreated to a gully behind the redoubt which they defended and where they received some reinforcement from their reserve. The Danes continued the attack and also took the gully. The Danish workforce immediately started to demolish the redoubt and burn the wood used as support in the earthwork. After the demolition had been carried out, the sortie commando and workforce retreated back into Fredericia.

When the Schleswig Holstein reinforcement arrived they discovered that the redoubt had been destroyed so they immediately began reconstruction. The redoubt, which later would be known as the 'Trelle redoubt' was completed as well as the two small artillery foundations further behind. Guns from this location made life difficult for the patrolling gun barges.

From the middle of May and throughout June, General Bülow and the Secretary of War corresponded and had several conferences where the future army operations were discussed.

Bülow envisaged several opportunities:

    Reinforcement of General Rye's corps
    Reinforcement of the Helgenæs redoubt
    Reinforcement of Fredericia and landing of troops nearby
    Various operations in Schleswig in order to disturb the enemy supply lines

The information on the German position and strength was, in May, incomplete although this improved as General Rye's intelligence organisation started working. The lack of information caused the Secretary of War and General Bülow to be hesitant in making any final decisions, however Bülow eventually became convinced by the reports he received from Colonel Lunding that the best place to perform an operation would be Fredericia.

The Secretary of War visited the fortress on 20th May just when the first artillery duels were concluded. This did not convince him that the time had come. On a meeting with Bülow it was decided to draw Rye's brigade towards Helgenæs with the view to ship four battalions and a battery of guns of the brigade to Funen and leave the Cavalry Brigade with two battalions behind. Transfer of troops from Als was also discussed.

General de Meza had 15,000 men on Als and was obliged to transfer one brigade (5,000 men) to Funen. De Meza was not happy with this arrangement which would weaken the defence of Als. Nevertheless the transfer would happen.

The Secretary of War was convinced that the sortie from Fredericia should take place from a reinforced garrison; Rye's brigade should land north of the fortress while General de Meza's brigade would land south of Frederica. In this way it would be possible to surround the Schleswig Holstein army. Bülow was against such a landing operation on the open beach because it demanded many more transport boats than were available. The landing boats could only transport one company at a time and therefore took too long, giving the Schleswig Holstein army the opportunity to neutralise the landing force.

During May General Bülow gave permission to carry out the attack from Fredericia and on 20th June General de Meza received the order to ship the 6th Brigade and a gun battery to Funen. General Rye was asked to have his four battalions ready on short notice and on 30th June the battalions and one gun battery was transported from Helgenæs to Funen.

At a conference between Colonel Lunding and General Bülow in Fredericia on 2nd July it was decided to undertake the sortie from Fredericia in the night between 4th–5th July. The commanding generals held conferences on 2nd and 4th July in order to sort out the details of the operation.

The landing of units south and north of Fredericia was finally abandoned on the advice from the Navy. It would therefore be a combined sortie of all the Danish units assembled in Fredericia. The 6th Brigade could not meet the schedule and the operation was therefore delayed for 24 hours.

The transfer of troops mostly took place during the night as it was hoped that the morning fog would conceal the activity. This turned out to be impossible and the Schleswig Holstein units quickly became aware of the activity. In response General Bonin ordered his artillery to shoot at the transport ships, nearly causing a disaster on 5th July. General Bülow and his staff were being transported to Fredericia on that day. Upon landing a shell exploded nearby. If it had hit, the entire staff could have been killed and the operation would have been without leaders. On 5th July all units were transported to Fredericia and some 23,000 troops were assembled inside the ramparts. At 01.00 hrs the Danish army surged out of the fortress and the attack began.

On the German side General Bonin had underestimated the strength of the Danish army in Fredericia. He did not know that General Rye had been transferred to Funen with part of his brigade. General Prittwitz learned about this from a deserter but it was too late. Bonin was aware of his exposed situation and was considering a retreat though he understood that this would have been terrible for the morale of his army. He decided to stay in the prepared positions and receive the Danish attack. His army was on full alert expecting an attack on 5th July.

The Danish sortie was organised in four brigades (the 3rd, 4th, 5th and 6th) each with a field battery, two cavalry units and the reserve artillery. The vanguard consisted of the 6th Brigade with one field battery and ½ espignol battery under the command of General de Meza (map 14). The weather was quiet with a clear sky and a full moon. The sortie marched out of the King's Gate with the goal of separating the northern and western Schleswig Holstein units.

The 5th Brigade under the command of General Rye stormed out along the beach aiming at the northern Schleswig Holstein positions, the Trelle redoubt. The field artillery moved out of the King's Gate after de Meza's brigade had made its sortie as the gates constituted a bottleneck. De Meza's Brigade formed two lines. The left flank of the first line was, shortly after the sortie, engaged in fighting with the western Schleswig Holstein redoubts whereas the right flank of the line had little resistance and was able to push into the open country between the Schleswig Holstein positions. Despite this, the advance stopped in order not to lose the connection with the battalions coming from the rear.

The Schleswig Holstein skirmish line at the western positions consisted of six companies from the 2nd Brigade. The remaining part of the brigade was in the camp behind the line or in transfer between the lines and the camp. The Danes attacked the Schleswig Holstein trenches and after one and a half hours of fighting the trenches were taken and the skirmishers had withdrawn or been captured.

The battalions in the camp could hear the noise from the fighting but could not advance fast enough to save the redoubts and trenches.

General Rye's Brigade (5th Brigade) attacked the northern redoubts, which were defended by two companies. The attack came when the companies were in the process of being relieved by two other companies, hence the total strength of the defenders was doubled.

The remaining part of the Schleswig Holstein northern units were in the camp at Kirstinebjerg and the villages Egeskov and Vejlby both situated at Rands fjord. While the trenches were taken quickly the Trelle redoubt was stubbornly defended (figure 4.5). Therefore General Rye decided to have the battalions of the first line continue the forward move while the second line should attack the redoubt. It took two and a half hours to accomplish this with fierce fighting and considerable casualties.

The noise of the battle alerted the Schleswig Holstein units in the northern camps and two battalions from Kirstinebjerg moved towards the fighting only to encounter the Danish 1st Light Battalion of the 6th Brigade's right flank. This encounter stopped the Schleswig Holstein battalions and they never managed to help the units at the redoubt. Eventually the reinforcement from the Danish 5th Brigade came up and secured the line.

100 FIRST SCHLESWIG HOLSTEIN WAR

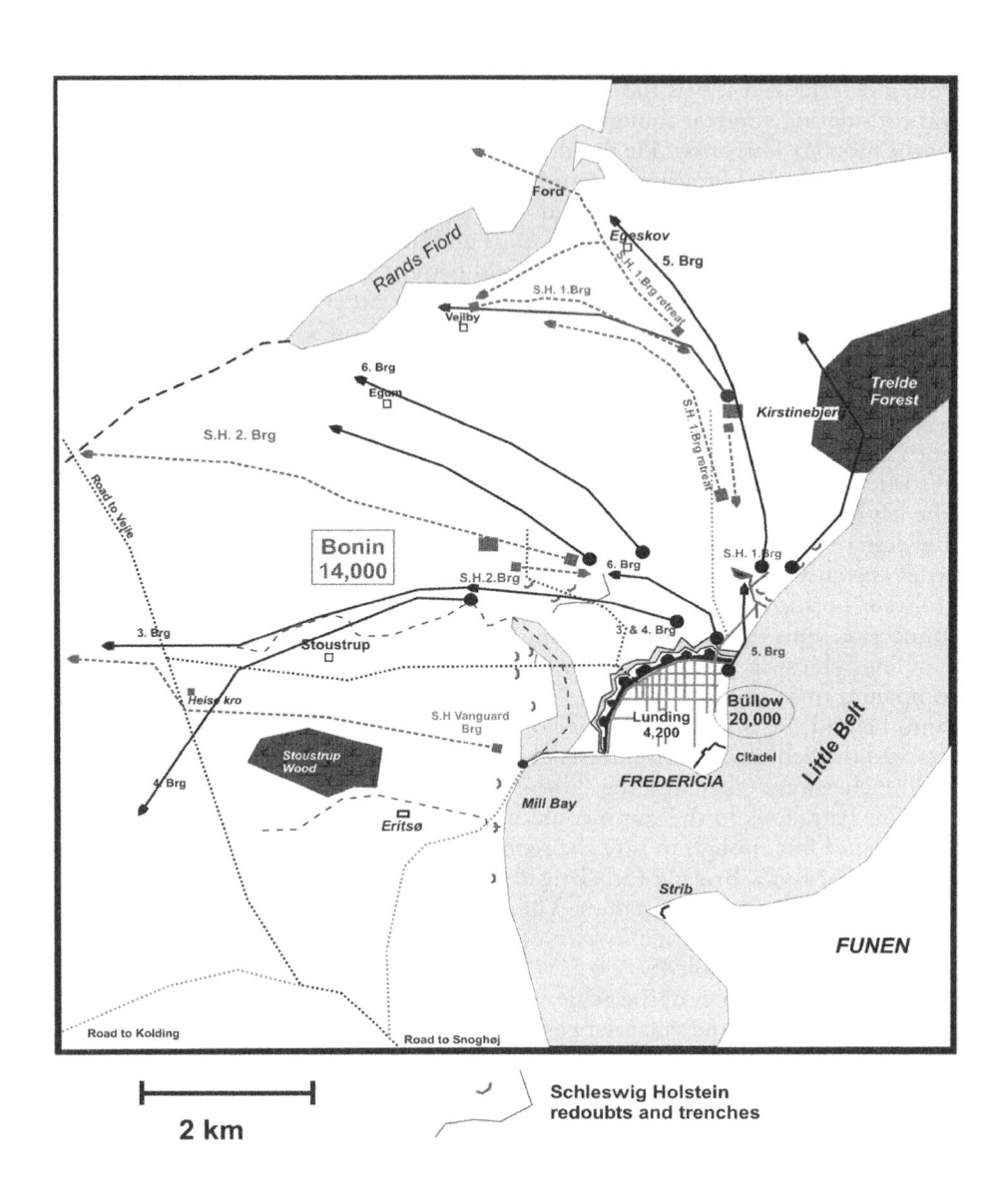

Map 14 Fredericia 6th July 1849

Figure 4.5 The fighting at the Trelle redoubt on 6th July 1849. The fighting took place in the dawn with only limited edition. The Schleswig Holstein soldiers could, however, fire at the dense columns of Danish soldiers. In the background are the ramparts of Fredericia.

The 6th Brigade's first line, consisting of two battalions, continued the move towards the Schleswig Holstein Redoubt III, which was situated some 400 m behind the western trenches and forward gun batteries. During the attack the Schleswig Holstein reinforcement of two Schleswig Holstein battalions assaulted and forced the Danish battalions into retreat. However, when the retreating troops met the second Danish line of the 6th Brigade they stopped.

Simultaneously, the 3rd Brigade under General Schleppegrell and the 4th Brigade under General Moltke had moved outside the ramparts of Fredericia. The 3rd marched through the King's Gate and a smaller gate next to the Queen's Bastion and the 4th along the beach.

The 3rd Brigade pushed forward between the flooded area and the Schleswig Holstein trenches. This and the renewed attack from 6th Brigade forced the Schleswig Holstein units into retreat.

It was at this time that General Bonin gave the order for a full retreat of the Schleswig Holstein army.

On the northern front the 5th Brigade's first line continued to push forward and forced the Schleswig Holstein battalion into retreat to Kirstinebjerg where it met the Schleswig Holstein reserves on their way to the front.

At 04.00 hrs, the Trelle redoubt was finally taken. It had been defended by only about 200 men and these were taken prisoner. During the final phase of the fighting at '*Trelle skansen*' General Rye had been riding into the front line. He was alone as his staff and aids were sent out on various task. During this ride he was killed (figure 4.6).

Figure 4.6 The death of General Rye at the Trelle redoubt.

The commanding officer of the northern Schleswig Holstein units gave the order to retreat. His reserve acted as the rearguard while he was rallying the remaining part of his force. He decided to retreat along the southern edge of Rands fjord. He had received information that Danish gun barges were positioned at the entrance to the fjord and that Danish forces had landed at the Trelle peninsula north of Fredericia.

The report of the landing troops was not correct but a battalion of General Rye's Brigade had the task of scouring the beach and clearing the Trelle peninsula of enemy troops. The scout information that the Schleswig-Holstein CO received was probably the movement of that battalion.

One of the Schleswig Holstein gun batteries escaped over the shallow water of Rands fjord but the rest of the Schleswig Holstein northern units retreated along the southern edge of Rands fjord and there met the Danish 6th Brigade, which had reached Egum and Bredstrup and in this way blocked the retreat. This caused confusion and the Schleswig Holstein units turned around and moved back to the fjord. Unfortunately the 5th Danish Brigade had arrived and now blocked this route. Only half of the Schleswig Holstein northern brigade escaped. The remainder were either killed or taken prisoner.

On the western front the Schleswig Holstein 2nd Brigade and Vanguard Brigade were in the process of retreating.

General Schleppegrell's 3rd Brigade, which was moving west, made a turn to the left towards Heise Inn. The 4th Brigade under General Moltke followed as reserve.

At around 17.00 hrs the Schleswig Holstein army stood at a line from Egum to Stovstrup putting up resistance but the continued attack from the Danish army forced General Bonin to order a full retreat and he decided that his army should move to Vejle. The Schleswig Holstein 2nd Brigade and the remnants of the 1st moved over the village Bredstrup towards the west crossing the Elbo valley while the Vanguard Brigade escaped to Havreballe village and by the evening they had reached Vejle, where they camped.

At the end of the battle the Danish army controlled the area between the Elbo valley and the coast. The Elbo valley is a wet area with a stream, only passable with heavy equipment such as cannons via some few fords, or bridges, and so it can easily be defended.

The Schleswig Holstein army suffered casualties of some 3,000 men, of whom 1,000 were dead or wounded and the rest became prisoners, i.e., a loss of 22%. Also, the Danes captured all their heavy siege guns as well as a good number of vehicles and field guns. The Danes had suffered 1,800 casualties, who were mostly dead and wounded, while hardly any had been taken prisoner.

At night the Danish army pulled back to Fredericia leaving only skirmishers on the battlefield. During the following days all the redoubts and trenches were destroyed. The significant higher casualties in dead and wounded for the Danish army was because they had to attack well prepared and defended positions.

The Armistice

Parallel to the warfare in Denmark, negotiations for a peace treaty took place in London. Both Britain and Russia had an interest in ending the war as their trade in the Baltic was suffering from the Danish naval blockade. The British Prime Minister, Lord Palmerstone, headed the negotiations and he proposed an armistice whereby there should be a demarcation line from Flensburg in the east to Husum in the west in order to separate the two parties. This was rejected by the Prussian negotiator.

In the Parliament in Frankfurt a new constitution for the entire 'Reich' was adopted during March 1849. The King of Prussia, Friedrich Wilhelm IV, was elected as Emperor of Germany though he refused this position in April and would not recognise the constitution, as it was too liberal. Austria, Saxon, Hanover and Bavaria refused as well. Friedrich Wilhelm then invited governments from various German states to come to Berlin to negotiate a new constitution. This resulted in rebellions in several places in Germany. The local governments tried to suppress the revolts but not always with success.

King Friedrich Wilhelm was also under pressure from the conservative parties to avoid supporting the liberal Schleswig Holstein constituencies. When the Prince of Nör resigned from the '*Statholderskab*' in Schleswig Holstein only the liberals remained in power and this liberalism was contrary to what King Wilhelm was trying to achieve in Prussia. In November 1848 the Prussian army crushed a liberal revolt in Berlin. Given the situation Prussia needed to have the army at home to fight possible revolutions.

Therefore in the middle of May in 1849 Prussia initiated negotiations with Denmark again, this time in Berlin. The negotiator from Denmark was the Lord in waiting Reedtz and from Prussia, Freiherr Schleinitz. The British ambassador in Berlin, Lord Westmoreland, was mediator.

The negotiations were slow but with the various revolts in Germany in mind Prussia made an armistice proposal in the middle of June. The proposal was not satisfactory to the Danes but better than what had been proposed earlier. The Danish Government was not inclined to accept and informed Reedtz about its decision.

Reedtz dared not inform the Prussian negotiator about this. On 3rd July Reedtz learned that a Russian courier was travelling to Copenhagen with a message from the Russian Foreign Secretary to the Danish Government. The message was that the Russian Government wanted the Danes to accept the Prussian armistice proposal. The courier travelled through Berlin and the Prussians succeeded in copying the message. Reedtz discovered this and felt it was time to react quickly even if he had to go beyond his instructions. He proposed some minor changes to the armistice which he had already negotiated and agreed to with Freiherr Schleinitz.

Reedtz demanded that the changes be accepted within 72 hrs. The proposal was debated in the Prussian Government and eventually accepted. On 8th July Reedtz learned about the decision in the Prussian Government but also about the Danish victory at Fredericia. He knew that when it became public that the Danes had beaten the Schleswig Holstein Army, the armistice could be in danger. He quickly arranged a meeting with Freiherr Schleinitz and with Lord Westmoreland as witness; the two negotiators signed the armistice proposal and peace preliminaries. The only thing missing was ratification by the two governments. The Prussian government signed on 10th July, 1849 after the victory at Fredericia became common knowledge.

This situation gave way to a lot of indignation in Germany and it is probable that Freiherr Schleinitz, the Prussian negotiator, would not have signed if he had known what had happened at Fredericia.

The Danish Government, after heated debate, ratified the armistice thus bowing to the Russian pressure. Secretary of War, Hansen tried to resign, but the Danish King refused, but also told him that he was relieved from the responsibility for the ratification. The rest of the Danish government agreed to the decision to ratify the armistice and this was accomplished on 15th July and on the 17th the ratified notes were exchanged in Berlin.

The Provisional Government in Schleswig Holstein was concerned about these negotiations in Berlin. An emissary from the Schleswig Holstein Provisional Government returned with reassuring messages about the implications of the agreement from the Prussian Government. Therefore the actual armistice came as quite a shock. Attempts were made to try to get the Prussian Government to annul the armistice but in vain. There was no help from the parliament in Frankfurt. There were then efforts to get the Prussian officers in Schleswig Holstein inclusive of General Bonin to continue the war.

General Prittwitz informed the Schleswig Holstein *Statholderskab* that if they resisted the armistice all Prussian officers would be pulled back immediately. The Schleswig Holstein population could do nothing to change the situation and on 24th July the German troops began their march home.

The duration of the terms for this armistice was for six months with a possibility for a six week extension. The southern part of Schleswig to a line south of Flensburg and north of Tønder would be controlled by 6,000 Prussian troops, and the northern part of Schleswig by 2,000 neutral Swedish troops. The Danes remained on the island of Als. The naval blockade would end and prisoners of war be exchanged.

A commission of three people was given the power to stop or ratify what was proposed by the '*Statholderskab*'. The commission would have a Danish, Prussian and British member, the latter as mediator.

There was also a secret part in the armistice agreement which allowed the Danish King to use his army to force the Schleswig Holsteiners to obey the armistice. If they did not obey and the Danish army had to come in, it was made clear that the Prussian army would withdraw.

The peace preliminaries included a separate constitution for Schleswig without breaking the ties to Denmark. The final set up would be negotiated with Britain as mediator. The Holstein and Lauenburg Duchies would stay in the German Confederation and likewise have a new constitution.

The issues with the royal succession in Denmark were discussed as well.

After the armistice was in place the Schleswig Holsteiners repeated what they had done the year before, they did not respect the conditions imposed up them and the commission of three people was never able to work.

The peace negotiations commenced in Berlin December 1849 but an impasse was quickly met. With the negotiation dragging out the conservative landlords of Schleswig Holstein became impatient. They were the main contributors to the war effort. During a meeting in Kiel on 6th April, 1850 they proposed that the '*Statholderskab*' initiated direct negotiations with the King of Denmark. The proposal was approved and a delegation went to Copenhagen on 18th April. The negotiations proved unsuccessful.

At the same time (17th April) Prussia made a proposal for a 'simple' peace whereby Prussia did not support Schleswig Holstein any more, but reserved its right in the Duchies.

The negotiations continued during the following months but with no results and the Danish Government decided to stop the negotiations and move into the Duchies in accordance with the secret agreement with Prussia.

Russia demanded that the Danes make one more attempt for a negotiated peace. They also proposed that the British Government carry out a naval demonstration against Prussia. Britain did not agree to this but it impressed Prussia. So on 4th July it signed a peace treaty with Denmark.

According to this treaty both countries retained their rights in the Duchies. The Danish King could thus demand the German Confederation to help him restore his legal power in Schleswig Holstein. If the Confederation decided not to help, the Danish King had the right to move into the Duchies without German intervention.

According to the treaty the Prussian army would move out of Schleswig within 11 days and Holstein not later than 22 days.

The Schleswig Holstein Provisional Government was aware of the situation and looked for a replacement for General Bonin. They succeeded in hiring the retired Prussian General Willisen. They did not succeed in replacing all the

Figure 4.7 **Carl Wilhelm von Willisen (1790–1879)** was from Prussia. He commanded the Schleswig Holstein Army at the battle at Isted and until the end of 1850.

Prussian officers who had served in the Schleswig Holstein army. On 8th April they announced the replacement of General Bonin with General Willisen.

Carl Wilhelm von Willisen (1790–1879) was from Prussia (figure 4.7). He had participated in the Napoleonic wars and later been tutor at the military academy in Berlin. He had been in Austrian service in Tyrol and Italy. In 1848 he was in charge of the local Government in Poznan with the task to mediate between the German and Polish population. He had not performed this task very well and was discharged in disgrace.

In 1850 he accidentally met a representative of the '*Statholders*' from Schleswig Holstein and was offered the charge as commanding general of the Schleswig Holstein Army, a position which he accepted.

General Willisen reorganised the Schleswig Holstein army because of the lack of officers. He increased the size of the battalions to 1,280 men and formed an army consisting of 20 battalions grouped into five brigades. The reorganised army did not have time for training before the initiations of hostilities hence the troops were not familiar with their battalion commanders and vice versa, a situation which can be vital in stressed battle situations.

Chapter 5

1850

The Battle at Isted

The Schleswig Holstein army was under the command of General Willisen and had, on the 14th of July, taken up positions at Isted with a strength of 27,000 men in five brigades.

The Danish army with General Krogh as Supreme Commander moved on 16th July into the Duchy of Schleswig with the first stop at Flensburg where the headquarters was set up. Both General Bülow and General de Meza had both been offered the command but refused due to illness.

Secretary of War, General Hansen felt himself obliged to give the command to General Krogh though he wanted to take the position himself. However, the Cabinet and the King were against it and he had to remain behind in Copenhagen.

By the time Krogh had set up his headquarters General de Meza was fully recovered from his illness and followed the army as an attached officer. General Krogh had divided his army into two divisions and now had the strength of 39,000 men.

It was a very sunny and warm July and during the march the soldiers suffered several casualties due to heat stroke. On 20th July reconnaissance units were sent south from Flensburg to engage the Schleswig Holstein troops along the main road to the town of Schleswig.

These units consisted of four battalions, three of which followed the main road and the fourth the road to Mysunde. The idea was to probe the Schleswig Holstein Army to find its position. All indications were that it was assembled at Isted. On 23rd July in the evening General Krogh met with his division commanders and six brigade commanders at Bilskov some six km south of Flensburg. One of the issues was to discuss the battle readiness of the army after the march in the hot weather. After consultation it was decided to advance on 24th July and attack on the 25th.

On the 24th, the Danish army moved south (map 15). The 1st Division travelled along the road to the town of Schleswig and at 05.00 hrs reached Stenderup where Willisen's army was observed in a forest called West Wood. The division immediately attacked the Schleswig Holsteiner's advanced brigade, which was forced to retreat south to a small stream, called Helligbæk.

The 2nd Division of the Danish army went along the road to Mysunde and at 08.00 hrs it reached Hostrup where it was to support the attack of the 1st Division.

General Krogh kept the 5th Brigade as reserve at the town of Stenderup. He and his headquarters went from Flensburg to southern Smedeby during the morning. It had been decided to try to surround the Schleswig Holstein army and so 3rd Brigade, commanded by Colonel Schleperen, marched west of the river

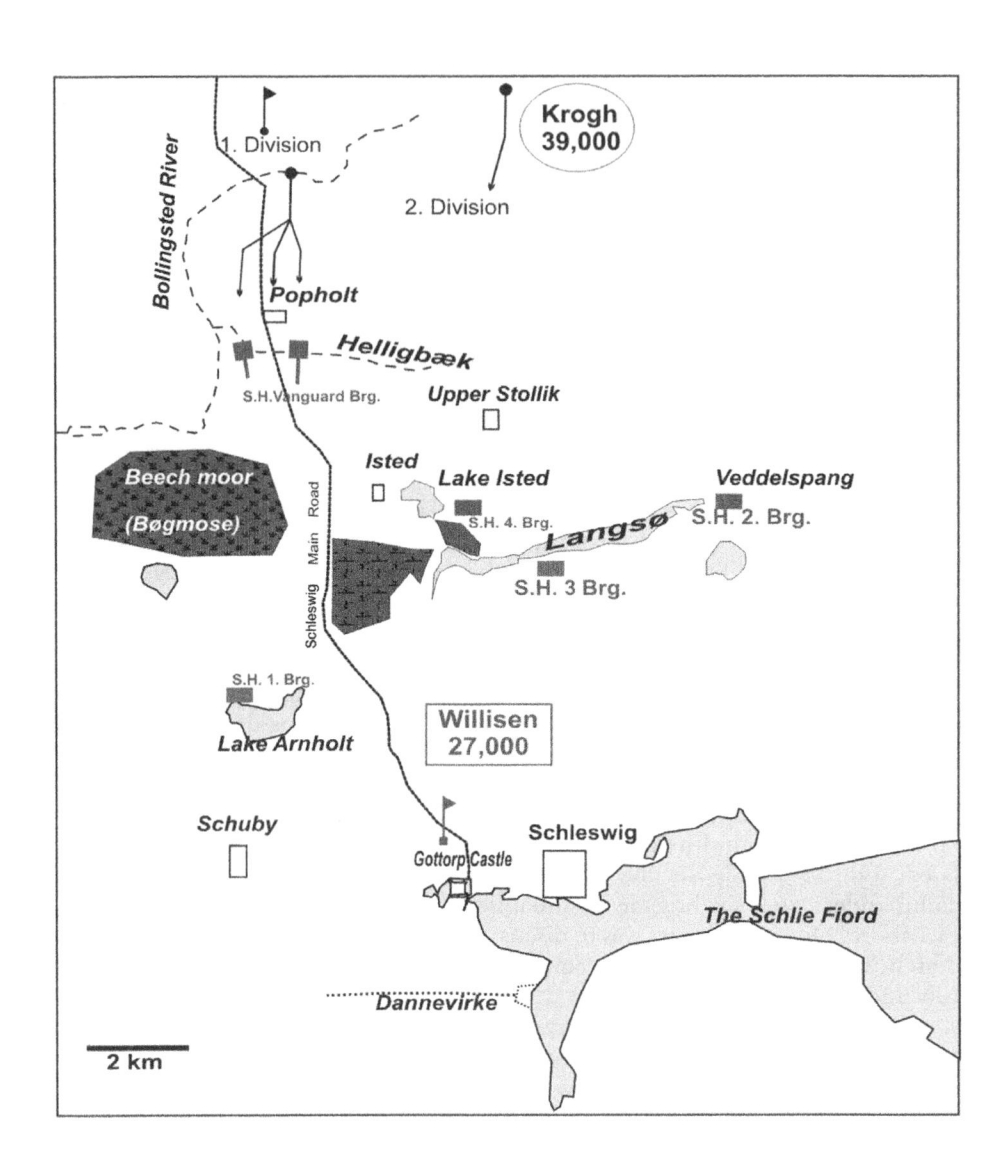

Map 15 Isted 24th July 1850

Trenen via Jørl Church to Solbro. It was then planned to back over the river to the eastern side in order to launch a flanking attack.

By 25th July the weather had changed, it was now raining and foggy. The gunpowder used in 1850 produced a lot of smoke when fired. The combination of powder smoke and fog made the visibility very poor over the battlefield. The commanding generals had visibility problems and the brigade commanders often lost contact with their battalions.

General Krogh's plan required an early attack at dawn. The two Danish divisions therefore pitched camp at 02.00 hrs (map 16). The 5th Brigade was ordered to form the first line. By 03.30 hrs the Brigade was ready at Helligbæk. The battalions of the Brigade totalled 6,000 men and were formed in a one km long front 100 to 300 m wide. After a move forward of some 200 m, the Danes met the Schleswig Holstein skirmish line and the battle at Isted had commenced.

The 6th and 4th Brigades, which had pitched camp at Stenderup West Wood, pushed forward. The 6th Brigade followed the main road after the 5th Brigade whereas the 4th Brigade marched along a side road west of the Schleswig main road. In total some 16,500 men were with the attacking brigades.

General Willisen on the other hand, had planned his attack for 04.00 hrs with the signal for the attack to be the ignition of bonfires. The order for this signal was issued at 04.45 hrs but due to the weather conditions not all units could see the bonfires, so the Schleswig Holstein attacks did not occur simultaneously.

Figure 5.1 General Frederik Adolf Schleppegrell (1792–1850) was born in Norway and participated as lieutenant in the resistance against the Swedes in 1814. He decided to leave Norway as he did not want to serve the Swedish king, who became king of Norway in 1814. Schleppegrell served in the Danish army until he was killed at Isted in 1850.

110 FIRST SCHLESWIG HOLSTEIN WAR

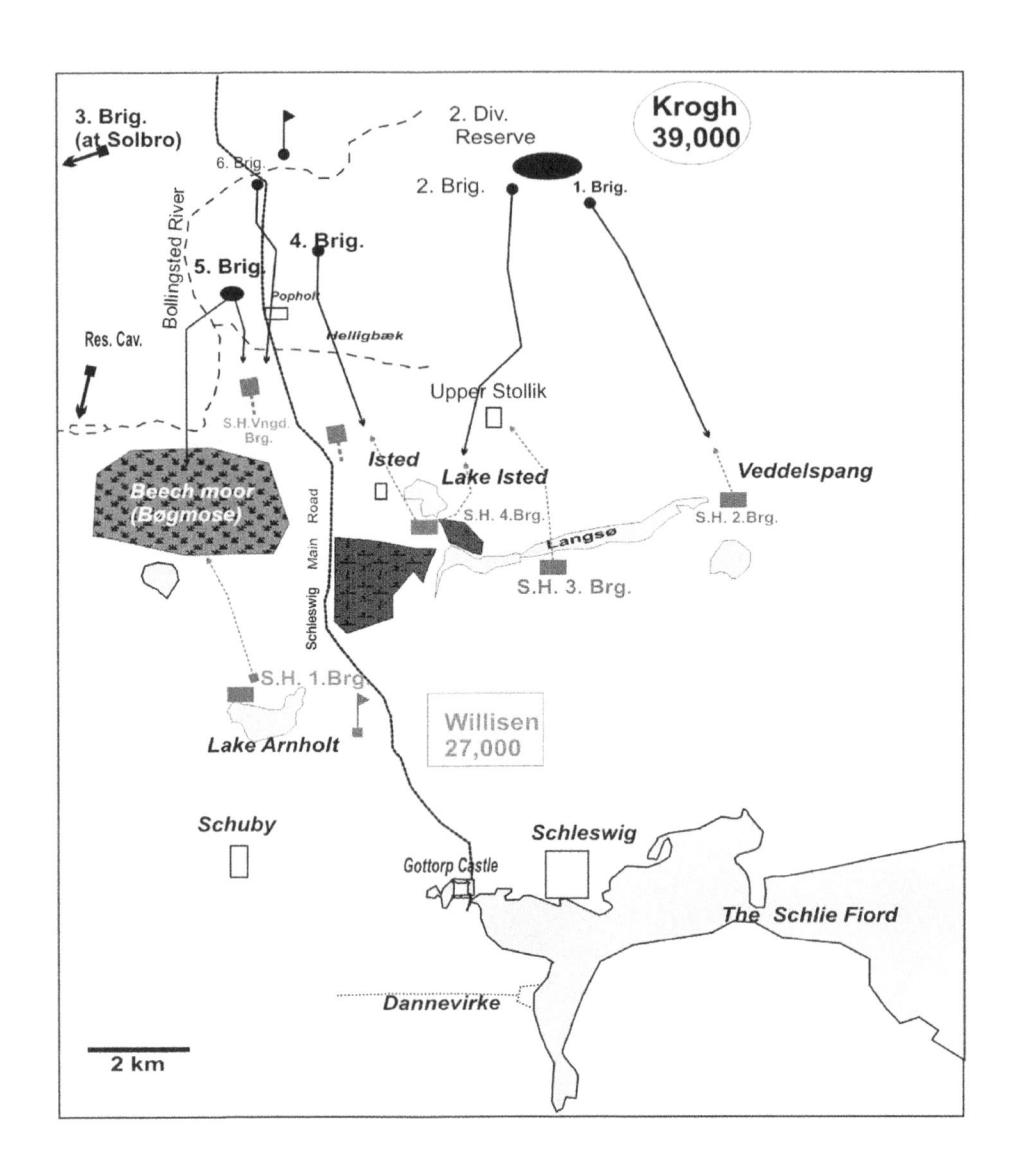

Map 16 Isted 25th July 1850 until 9 a.m.

The Danish 5th Brigade went west of the road and into a boggy area called Bøgsmosen. In this area fierce fighting took place with the Schleswig Holstein units, which lasted for four to five hours. A clay pit in the north-western edge of the boggy area was captured at 04.30 by the Danes.

The Schleswig Holstein vanguard brigade was forced to retreat to the other side of the bog where it received support from the Schleswig Holstein 1st Brigade. The Danes were then forced to retreat. During subsequent hours the clay pit changed hand six times. At around 07.00 hrs the Schleswig Holstein Brigade was in retreat and at 09.00 hrs they were at a position around Lake Arnholdt. The fighting was bloody as can be envisaged from the casualty list – the Danish 5th Brigade lost 16% of its men in dead and wounded. Only the Danish 2nd Brigade suffered higher casualties.

The Danish 2nd Division under General Schleppegrell (figure 5.1) commenced the advance at 01.30 hrs from the camp at Havetofte. Part of the 1st Brigade under Colonel Krabbe took the road to Mysunde which heads towards the eastern end of Lake Langsø, where the brigade encountered the Schleswig Holstein 2nd Brigade commanded by Colonel Abercron.

The 2nd Brigade of the 2nd Danish Division marched along the road to Upper Stolk and Isted. General Krogh had asked General Schleppegrell to move quickly, because the fighting at the Schleswig main road had commenced earlier than expected. Colonel Læssøe commanded the first battalions, which went through Upper Stolk village. Two of the battalions made it to the eastern end of Lake Isted and were quickly involved in the fighting of the 1st Division and it was here that Colonel Læssøe was killed.

Figure 5.2 The battle at the village of Isted 1850. The Schleswig Holstein soldiers defended the village fiercely. The Danes succeeded in setting the houses on fire using rockets, forcing their opponents into retreat.

By 05.00 hrs, the 3rd Schleswig Holstein Brigade had spotted the bonfire signal and had passed over the bridge which they had constructed at Lake Langesø and hurried towards Upper Stolk. About 06.00 hrs, while part of the Danish 2nd Division moved through the village, the Schleswig Holstein Brigade attacked scattering the Danish troops. General Schleppegrell (map 16) tried to rally them without success. Instead he assembled some cavalry troops and together attacked along a road which leads out of the village towards the south. During this attack he was killed. The road still exists and there is a small monument where the General was killed. The road is flanked by earth walls even today; it was simply suicide to attack in such a place. The enemy soldiers only needed to jump over the wall to take cover and enfilade the attacking cavalry.

With the commanding general dead, confusion arose among the Danish troops. The Brigade CO, Colonel Baggesen, escaped to Isted where he tried to rally his scattered men. He sent messages to the Supreme Command with information about the situation at Upper Stolk which by 07.00 hrs was very critical for the Danes. The reserve of the 2nd Division had been delayed. It was under the command of Colonel Henckel. He observed the fighting at a distance and therefore had his battalions prepare for an attack. The scattered troops he met were rallied and half an hour later he had forced the Schleswig Holstein units out of Upper Stolk and they retreated to the bridge over Lake Langesø. The situation was now under control for the Danes.

The Supreme Command who had received the bad news ordered two battalions to Upper Stolk. Furthermore General de Meza (figure 5.3) who had followed the staff but with no command also went to Upper Stolk to take over the 2nd Division and try to get the situation under control. It took some time before he had a full overview. His first messages were not very optimistic but at about 10.00 hrs he had been in contact with Colonel Henckel and could inform the Supreme Command that the front was stabilised.

During the critical period prior to 10.00 hrs General Krogh realised that he had only limited reserves left. He sent a message to the 3rd Brigade, which had passed west of the river Trenen in a flanking manoeuvre, that the Brigade should immediately retreat as it could be very exposed and it was needed as a reserve behind the main front.

As mentioned earlier the 4th Brigade had attacked Isted. The fighting at Isted was fierce and Isted village changed hands several times but around 10.00 hrs the defending 4th Schleswig Holstein Brigade had been driven out (figure 5.2).

At this point, the Danes now had the front stabilised from Isted to Bøgsmosen in the west. When the Supreme Command received these encouraging messages from the various commanders it was decided to launch the main attack. During the battle of the morning the various battalions had been scattered and mixed. It was therefore decided to reorganise the units prior to the main attack. In the meantime the artillery took over and from both sides guns exchanged cannonades.

The 3rd Danish Brigade under the command of Colonel Schleperen had marched south on the western side of the river Trenen. During the morning the brigade reached the bridge at Solbro, which was defended by Schleswig Holstein units. As the Danish troops arrived the Schleswig Holstein troops ignited the

Figure 5.3 **Christian de Meza (1792–1865)** was born in Ellsinore and joined the army in 1803 as a volunteer in the artillery. In 1808 he was made lieutenant. In the following years he served as teacher at the school of artillery. De Meza soon developed a very eccentric way of life - which he was well known for. In 1842 he became major and in 1848 he joined the artillery and was, shortly after the outbreak of the war, promoted to colonel. During the war he was known for his cool and calm behaviour in battle situations. All his eccentricity disappeared when the bullets flew around him. In 1849 he participated in the battles at Sundeved and was appointed major general and commanding officer on Als. He was with the troops at the battle at Fredericia.

After the war he became general inspector for the artillery. He was part of the military commission who worked out the plans for the defences at Dybbøl, Dannevirke and Fredericia in 1855 to 1857. In 1858 he was commanding general in Schleswig and in 1863 commanding general in Copenhagen. At the outbreak of the war in 1864 he was given the supreme command of the Danish Army. It was the wishes of the King, and the Secretary of War had to obey. De Meza was not popular in Copenhagen when he made decided to order the retreat of the Danish Army from the Dannevirke. He and his Chief of Staff were called to Copenhagen where he was exposed not only to the anger of the Secretary of War but to criticism in the newspapers. He was dismissed and given the task as commanding general in Copenhagen. In turn, he completely withdrew from all public appearance and died in 1865, probably of grief. Prior to his death he made a written statement concerning his conduct of war which was published after his death. It shows that he was mentally sharp and clear and not affected by his age.

bridge. Nevertheless the Danish soldiers were able to put out the fire. The defending troops retreated.

The Danish engineers quickly laid out a floating bridge, which had been part of the 3rd Brigade's equipment, and the old bridge was repaired. Therefore at 05.00 hrs the Brigade could cross the river unscathed and walk towards Schuby, experiencing minor skirmishes with the Schleswig Holstein 1st Brigade. At around 12.00 hrs the Danish Brigade was at Schuby, which is some four km west of Schleswig town and immediately behind the main front of the Schleswig Holstein army.

Colonel Schleperen instructed his artillery to fire a volley in order to let the Danish army know his position. At the same time he received the message from General Krogh to retreat. Schleperen obeyed the order as the good soldier he was and the message could not be misunderstood. The 3rd Brigade therefore retreated along the same route it had marched the whole morning on the western side of the river Trenen.

General Willisen was of the opinion at 06.00 hrs that there was still a good chance for a victory, however as the fighting developed and his troops were forced further and further back he decided to retreat. He had still not received any alarming news of large formations of Danish troops to the west so when the fighting at Isted became quieter and while the Danes were regrouping he postponed the decision to retreat. However, when he received the news about the cannonade of the 3rd Danish Brigade around 12.00 hrs he realised that a large Danish unit was present immediately in his rear that could block his retreat route. As his infantry was becoming weary after the fighting during the whole morning he gave the order for a general retreat (map 17).

At the same time the Danish main attack commenced. The 6th Brigade struck along the Schleswig main road and at Isted the 4th and 2nd Brigades attacked. During the retreat of the Schleswig Holstein army some of its units panicked caused by the retreating artillery, which drove into some of the marching infantry units. The Schleswig Holstein army pulled back to the town of Schleswig where it assembled before moving south to Rendsburg.

The marching route was through a landscape which did not favour cavalry attack. The Danish 3rd Brigade had progressed northward and was no hindrance to the retreat. The Danish reserve cavalry pursued the Schleswig Holstein army but was not able to cause any harm at all. The Danish infantry were so exhausted after the fighting that it was not able to follow up on its advantage. It just walked slowly after the Schleswig Holstein army to the south and at night took up positions at the old Dannevirke rampart.

The battle at Isted was over; it is the larges land battle which has taken place in the Nordic countries ever. The Schleswig Holstein army had 1327 dead and wounded and 1501 taken as prisoners by the Danes. The Danish army had 3203 dead and wounded and 415 taken as prisoners of war.

The naval operations in 1850

With the peace between Prussia and Denmark it was not necessary to blockade the Prussian and German rivers. Therefore less ships were equipped in 1850. How-

CHAPTER 5: 1850   115

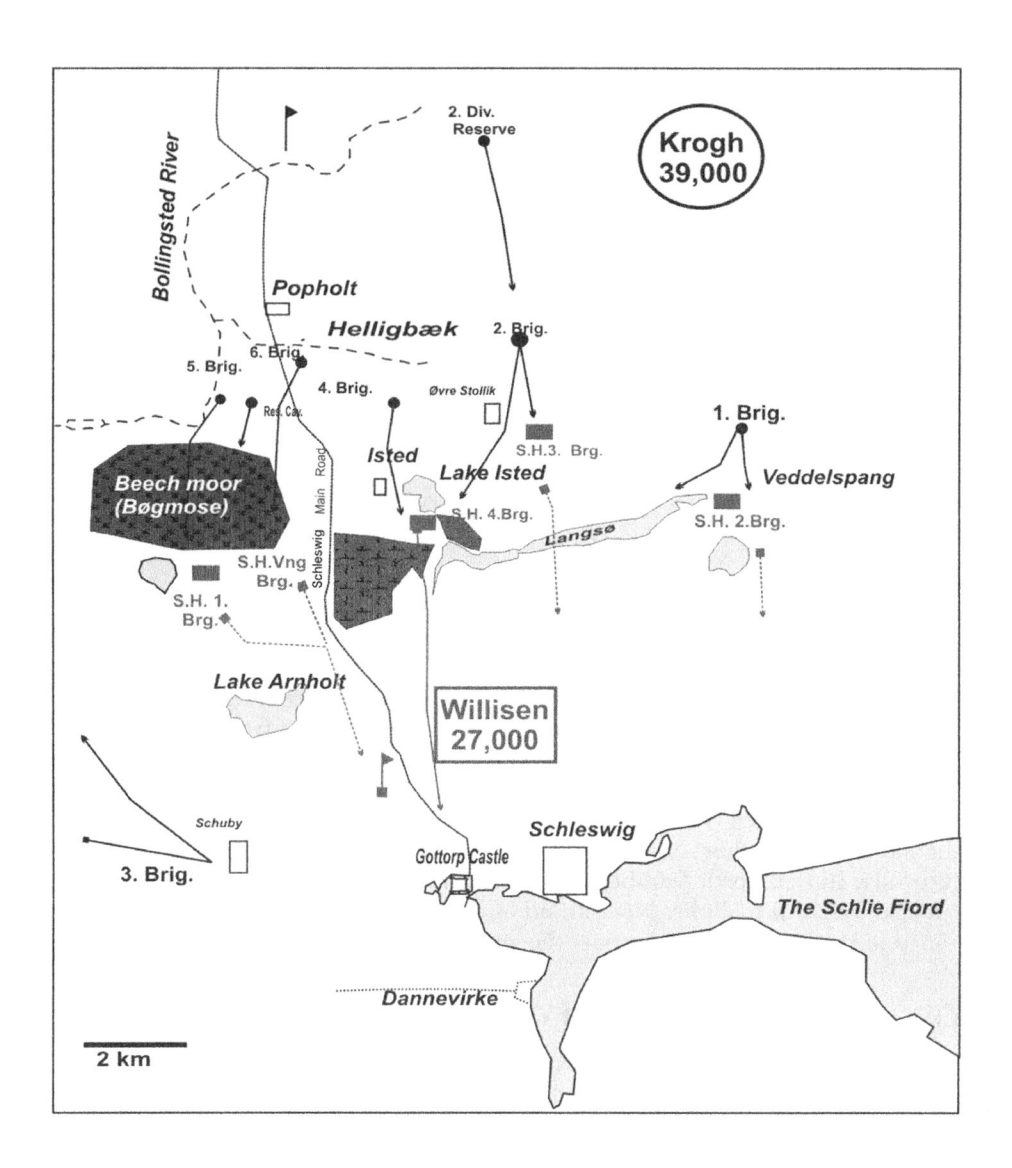

Map 17 Isted 25th July 1850 until 12 noon

Figure 5.5 Danish troops at the Dannevirke rampart. The field camp behind the rampart is typical for the field camps used by both armies. Often the local farmers also had to accommodate and supply the troops.

ever, a ship of the line and a steamer were sent to Kiel and four other larger ships supported by 4 gun barges were sent to Eckernförde. In addition to that 8 gun barges were sent to the Schlie fjord. Furthermore the ships *Ørnen* and *Saga* supported by 4 gun barges were sent to the islands of Fehmarn, which is part of the duchy of Holstein. On 17th July the island was occupied by troops landed from the ships. The ships *Valkyrien* and *Hekla* were sent to the Neustadt embayment to guard against the Schleswig Holstein ships that were stationed there. This included the steamer *Von den Tann*, which was chased into neutral harbour of Lübeck. However, it was not allowed to stay there and when it tried to escape it grounded and exploded on 20th July. In the North Sea there was skirmishing with small ships in the Vatten Sea at the islands of Föhr, Nordstrand and Pelvorn. The corvette *Flora* was stationed in the North Sea to support the gun barges' actions.

The period until the end of the war

The war continued for half a year after the battle at Isted. It was not until January 1851 that the Danish army went back to its barracks. The period from the battle at Isted to January 1851 was by no means quiet. There were several smaller battles and skirmishing. The battle for Friedrichstad and Jagel are examples. On average each day in the period a military encounter occurred.

The Danish army was now waiting on the Schleswig Holsteiners. It was not considered wise to enter into the Holstein Duchy in order not to violate any of the peace agreements. General Krogh should have said in this period: "Willisen is expecting us to attack but we are awaiting his attack. We will now see who can hold out for the longest period."

During this period, General Willisen believed that the Danish Army would attack Rendsburg and therefore initiated various construction works on the

CHAPTER 5: 1850   117

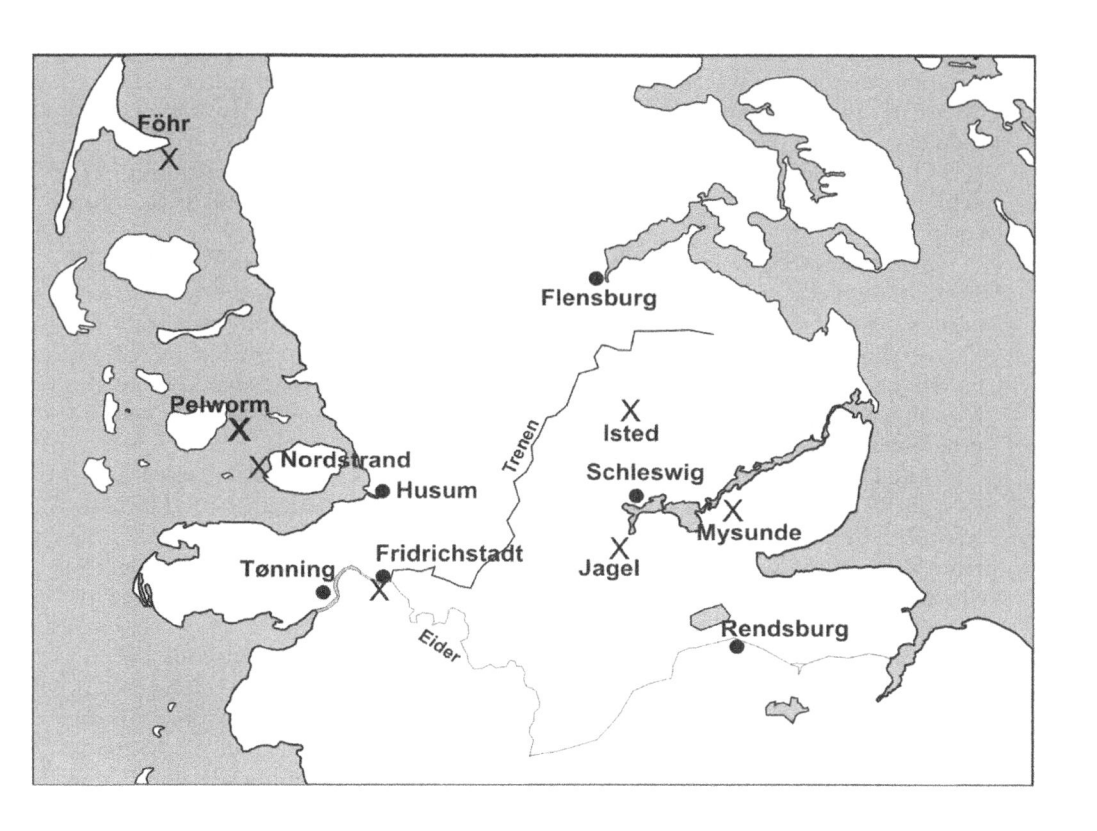

Map 18 Schleswig 1850 – battles and skirmishes

ramparts of the city and construction of new redoubts. The Provisional Government urged him to conduct more aggressive warfare but he was not inclined to do so. He tried to improve on the lack of officers by promoting the adjutants of the battalions, mostly lieutenants, and to get more volunteers from Germany. He was able to increase the Schleswig Holstein Army by some 7,000 men over the last part of 1850.

On 12th September, General Willisen attacked Mysunde at the fjord of the Schlie with a force of 17 infantry battalions, 10½ cavalry squadrons and 76 canons (map 18).

Mysunde was defended by the Danish 1st Brigade under Colonel Krabbe. The 1st Brigade had constructed some trenches around the village to defend this very narrow part of the fjord where it was possible to cross and thus penetrate the Danish line on the other side. Colonel Krabbe had positioned three of his battalions at the bridgehead with 10 canons. The position was attacked but the Danish battalions were able to resist and after some four hours of fighting with no progress General Willisen gave the order to stop and draw back.

The Danish Army had sent the 3rd Brigade under Colonel Schleperen to the west and occupied the village of Husum and the town of Friedrichstadt. The latter was taken by 1½ battalions commanded by Colonel Helgesen. It is situated at the river Eider in the wet area of the southernmost part of Schleswig surrounded by dikes and canals. The access is along roads on dikes. As was to be expected, the population in the town did not support the Danish King.

General Willisen decided to attack the town and therefore sent Colonel von der Tann with 2½ battalions (some 2,500 troops) to Friedrichstadt (map 19). On 29th September two groups attacked from the west, one along the road on the Eider dike and another on the Rendsburg road further inland. Due to the many ditches in the fields around the town the attack had to be conducted along these

Figure 5.4 A view of the battle at Friederichstadt, 4th October 1850. Colonel Helgesen, the commanding Danish officer, standing behind the ramparts.

CHAPTER 5: 1850   119

1 - Mill redoubt
2 - Gooshof
3 - Holmer Tor
4 - Trene redoubt
5 - Goldnes Tor

Ca. 500 m

Houses in Friedrichstadt
Gardens or vegetation
Ditch with water
Dike

Danish redoubt

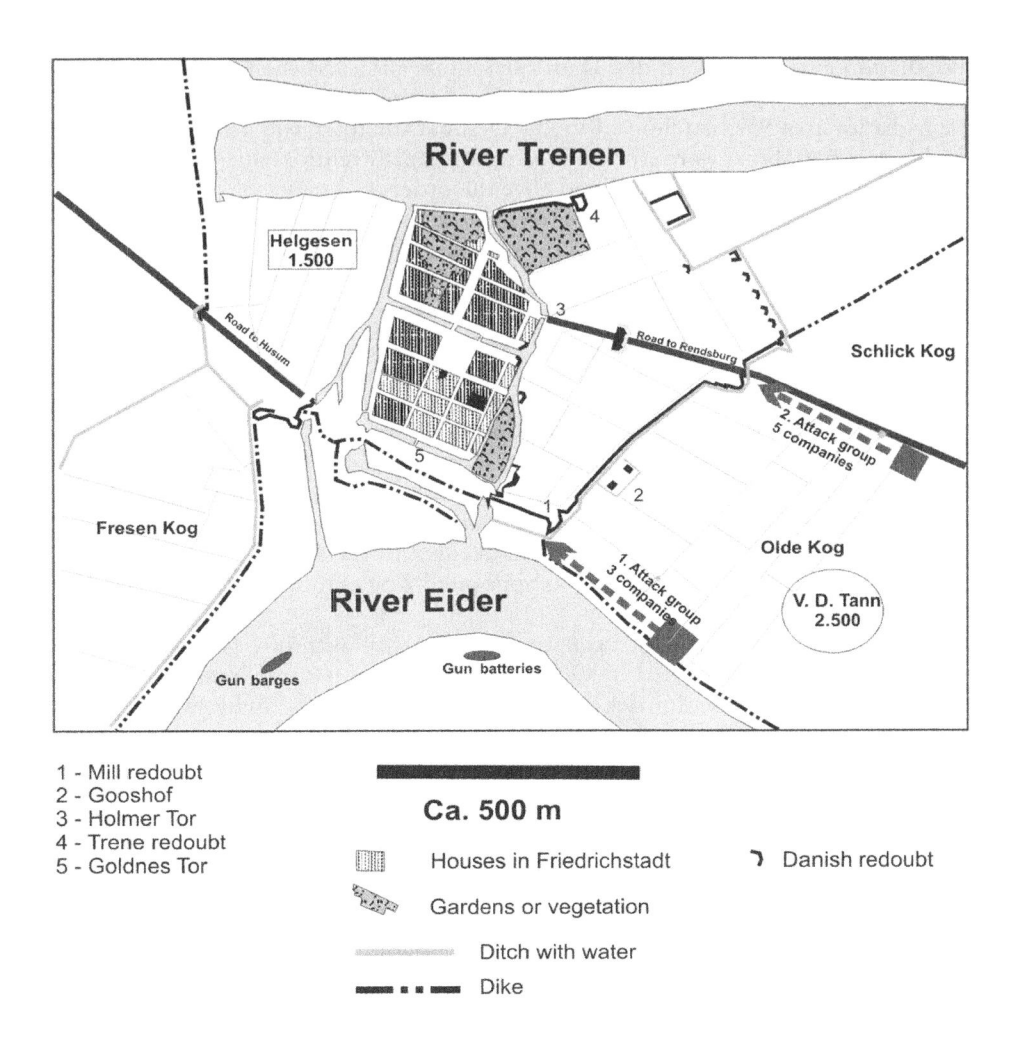

Map 19 Friederichstadt 27th September 1850

two routes. Artillery was placed on the southern side of the river opposite the town. The guns bombarded the Danish redoubts (figure 5.4) which were positioned on the roads to control the access to the town. In addition to the land-based cannons, two gun barges approached the town on the river.

Due to the heavy bombardment the Danish Colonel Helgesen had the civil population evacuated. Von der Tann's battalions attacked the Danes but did not succeed in taking the redoubts. Willisen therefore reinforced von der Tann so that he had a force of 9½ battalions. On 4th October the town was attacked again but Helgesen's battalions were still able to resist. Danish reinforcements were sent in and late in the day General Willisen gave the order to retreat.

During the rest of the year there were no major battles and only skirmishing.

The peace treaty of 2nd July required ratification from the German Confederation and this was difficult to accomplish. The Danish government was forced to negotiate with each of the 17 member states and not until September did Denmark succeed in getting each of the members to agree. Eventually on 26th October the peace treaty was ratified by the German Confederation.

One of the problems was that Prussia was not eager to force the Schleswig Holstein army to lay down their arms. On the other hand Austria, the other very influential member of the Confederation, was prepared for a military execution in Schleswig Holstein. However, Prussia was not eager to let Austrian troops into northern Germany an area it considered as its 'sphere of interest'.

On 7th December General Willisen decided to leave the Schleswig Holstein army and General von den Horst was appointed new commander. It was his plan to reactivate the war.

Prussia and Austria had been on the brink of war but had come to an agreement which was signed in Olmütz (present day name Olomouc) on 29th November. The two countries agreed to finally settle the Schleswig Holstein problem. The Russian Tsar had also put pressure on Prussia not to obstruct the German Confederation's military implementation.

The Schleswig Holstein provisional government was advised on 6th January that they should immediately stop fighting and reduce their army to one third. If the Provisional Government did not agree 25,000 Prussian and 25,000 Austrian soldiers would move over the river Elbe and force the Schleswig Holsteiners to obey. Von den Horst and his officers told the Provisional Government that they would not be able to fight both the Danish army and the combined Prussian and Austrian forces. The Provisional Government debated the issues and decided to leave the decision to the Schleswig Holstein Parliament.

During a meeting on 11th January 1851 in the parliament it was agreed to lay down arms. In the last counting of the Schleswig Holstein Army it had 860 officers and 43,288 soldiers of which some 3,000 were from the Confederation and 2,000 from Prussia. Most of the army was released and therefore on 18th January the Schleswig Holstein troops left Rendsburg with the exception of a minor garrison. In the subsequent weeks the soldiers were sent home and the army reduced to 13,000 men. This was in agreement with the treaty and the size was what Holstein and Lauenburg were required to have ready for the Confederation's army. The Danish troops occupied Rendsburg, and the Austrian army, the other larger towns in Holstein.

Denmark took over all the army equipment and naval ships. It included 645 cannon, 54,810 muskets, rifles and pistols, 42,660 sabres, 17,900 saddles and other cavalry equipment and a huge amount of ammunition.

On 26th January General Krogh held a major parade with a large contingent of the Danish army. Here after the Danish army were also reduced. The army of the line was sent back to its garrisons in Denmark while the reserve units stayed behind in Schleswig to keep the order.

The period after the war

At the end of the war the Danish army occupied the Duchy of Schleswig down to the river Eider and Rendsburg. The southern part of the Duchy was declared under martial law, which meant military control. Holstein continued to be occupied by the Austrian Army until the end of 1851 when it pulled out and the Danish Army moved in.

Negotiations between the various parties continued and eventually in 1852 Denmark declared that it would not include Schleswig in the Danish Kingdom nor would it include Holstein. Instead they would keep the Duchies and the Kingdom separate which satisfied Prussia and the German states.

Denmark tried in the following years to solve the constitutional problems but in vain. In 1861 it was even close to war again due to the various interferences from the German Federation.

The period was characterised by bitterness from the Schleswig Holstein population. The Danish policy in the area did not do anything to ease the situation by forcing the Danish language into schools and the church.

The Danish Government gave a general amnesty for the Schleswig Holstein soldiers. The members of the Provisional Government were not included in any amnesty and expelled from the Kingdom and the Duchies.

The Duke of Augustenburg, Christian August was expelled from Denmark and Schleswig Holstein 1851. The Danes considered the Duke's behaviour to have been treasonous. All his estates were confiscated although he was given a compensation of 3,650,000 *Rigsdaler*. He also had to sign a declaration promising never to go back to Denmark, that his children would never disturb the peace in Denmark and that he would never work against the royal succession in Denmark. Later, in 1864, the second Schleswig-Holstein war did not bring Christian August back to power, that was not included in the schemes set out by Bismarck.

The Prince of Nör did not have his estates confiscated but was expelled and had to live outside Denmark and Schleswig Holstein. He died in 1865 in Egypt.

The question of the royal succession was solved in 1851 by the election of Christian of Glücksburg as successor of Frederik VII. The Glücksburg family was related to the Danish royal family in the same manner as the Augustenborg family. Christian was the only of the Glücksburg family who had been loyal to the Danish King. As a cavalry officer he had participated in the war on the Danish side while his older brother had been officer in the Schleswig Holstein Army. His younger brothers had joined the Prussian army before the war. They managed to avoid service in Schleswig Holstein despite the battalions they served in being sent to

Denmark. The royal succession was confirmed by the great states of Europe at a conference in London in 1852.

There were others who decided to leave voluntarily. During the years after the war the emigration from the Duchies to the USA increased significantly. Some ten percent of the officers of the Schleswig Holstein army left for the USA.

After the war in 1864 when Prussia had conquered the Duchies it was the turn of the Danish speaking population to emigrate.

The 1848 to 1850 political situation was not solved and this was eventually used by the Prussian chancellor Bismarck to declare war on Denmark in 1864.

After that war the Duchies were finally ceded from Denmark, including the Danish speaking population. It was not until 1920 that the northern part of Schleswig, where the bulk of the Danish speaking people were living, was returned to Denmark after a referendum.

Appendix A
Statistical tables

Table 1 The maximum number of men under arms for the three years of war

Year	Denmark Total no.	Germany/Schleswig-Holstein Newly conscripted	The army in S.H. only
1848	27,000	14,000	70,000
1849	41,000	10,000	70,000
1850	41,000	11,000	42,000

Table 2 The Danish gun system of 1834

Type	Weight kg	No. of guns	Year of Manufacture	Place of Manufacture	Max range m
6 pound ball canon	395	194	1834–47	Åker	1255
12 pound howitzer	394	64	1834–46	Åker	1883
12 pound ball canon	781	147	1834–51	Åker	1569
24 pound howitzer	802	127	1834–51	Stafsiö	2197
24 pound ball canon	2209	126	1840–50	Åker Stafsiö	1569
84 pound howitzer	2216	130	1840–50	Finspong	3766
36 pound ball canon	3907	36	1844–45	Finspong Finspong & Stafsiö	1569
84 pound heavy howitzer	4254	147	1835–52		3766
168 pound howitzer	5228	19	1846	Stafsiö	1883
24 pound hand mortar	203	82	1841–42 & 51	Åker & Carlshütte	942
84 pound mortar	688	12	1841–42	Åker	1883
168 pound mortar	1067	38	1841 & 64	Åker & Finspong	1883

All the manufacturers are in Sweden. The number of guns is the number of guns manufactured between 1834 and 1864.

Table 3 The Royal Danish Navy in 1848

Type	Name	No of guns	Age (in 1848)**	Max (crew)	Active in 1848	Active in 1849	Active in 1850
Ships of the line	Danmark ***	66	31	696	—	—	—
	Waldemar (POW ship)	84	20	665	—	—	—
	Frederik VI	84	17	665	—	—	—
	Skjold	84	15	665	—	1	1
	Christian VIII	84	8	665	—	1	—
	Dannebrog (ready in 1850)	80	*	692	—	—	—
Frigates	Dronning Marie	84	24	665	—	—	—
	Nymphen	40	32	322	—	—	—
	Fylla	40	31	322	—	—	—
	Freja	46	29	404	1	—	1
	Rota	46	25	404	—	—	—
	Havfruen	46	22	404	1	1	—
	Bellona	46	17	404	1	1	—
	Thetis	48	8	404	1	—	1
	Gefion	48	4	397	1	1	—
	Tordenskjold (ready in 1852)	48	*	421	—	—	—
Corvettes	Najaden	20	28	130	1	1	—
	Flora	20	21	130	1	—	1
	Valkyrien	20	2	147	—	—	1
	Galathea	26	16	216	1	—	—
Barks	Saga (crew estimated)	12	*	70	—	—	1
Brigs	St. Croix	12	13	70	—	1	—
	Mercurius	12	11	70	1	1	—
	St. Thomas	16	21	91	1	1	—
	Ørnen	16	6	95	—	1	1
Schooners	Elben	8	16	53	—	—	—
	Pilen	2	16	17	—	—	—
	Delphinen	2	20	17	—	—	—

Type	Name	No of guns	Age (in 1848)**	Max (crew)	Active in 1848	Active in 1849	Active in 1850
Steam ships	Hekla	7	6	140	1	1	1
	Gejser	8	4	118	1	1	1
	Skirner	2	1	45	1	1	1
	Ægir	2	7	35	1	1	1
	Kiel	2	24	34	1	1	1
	Ejderen	4		30	—	—	1
Total Ships					15	15	13
Total Crew active					3022	3363	2317

* Being built in 1848
** Years
*** Placed in Copenhagen and used as POW ship

The Schleswig Holstein navy in 1850

Type	Name	No of guns	Build in year	Max crew
Frigates (captured from the Danes*)	Gefion	48	4	397
Cutter	Tummler	—	—	—
Schooners	Elbe **	8	—	—
Paddle Steam ships	Bonin	4	—	73
	Kiel **	4	—	34
	Löwe	—	—	40
	Rendsburg	—	—	—
	Eider	—	—	—
Screw steamer	v.d.Tann	2	1850	24

* Assigned to the Confederate Navy
** Captured from the Danish Navy but after war returned to Denmark

Table 4a Danish rowing gun barge squadron 1848–1850

Type	No.	Displacement in tons	Crew	No. of guns and type
Gun barges	5	38,7	64	2 18 pound
Gun barges	38	38,7	64	2 18 pound
				4 4 pound howitzer
Bombardment barge	23	48,7	64	1 60 pound bombardment cannon
				1 24 pound
				4 4 pound howitzer
Gun dinghy	4	11,1	24	1 24 pound
				1 4 pound howitzer
Bombardment dinghy	17	12,6	24	1 60 pound bombardment cannon
				2 4 pound howitzer

The gun barges were also used as transport vessels and 16 of them never came into action.

The bombardment barges were all used during the war. The gun dinghies were placed at Bornholm in the Baltic.

Table 4b Schleswig Holstein rowing gun barge squadron 1848–1850

Type	No.	Displacement in tons	Crew	No. of guns and type
Gun barges without deck	4		50	2 60 pound
Gun barges with deck	7		50	60 pound

The armament and displacement was probably the same as for the Danish gun barges

Table 5 Localities and alternative names

Danish	Type	Geographical location	German
Åbenrå	Town	North Schleswig	Apenrade
Adsbøl	Village	Sundeved peninsula	Arzbüll
Als	Island	East coast of north Schleswig	Alsen
Arnholt	Lake	North west of the town of Schleswig	Arenholz
Avnbøl	Village	Sundeved peninsula	Auenbüll
Bov	Village	North of Flensburg	Bau
Broager	Peninsula	South of Sundeved	Broacker
Bustrup	Village	South of the town of Schleswig	Bustorf
Dannevirke	Old rampart	South of the town of Schleswig	Danewerke
Dybbøl	Village	Sundeved	Düppel
Eckernførde	Town and bay	North west of Kiel	Eckernförde
Ejder	River and canal	Kiel to Tönning	Eider
Eritsø	Village	South of Fredericia	Eritsee
Fanø	Island	West coast of south Jutland	Fanö
Flensborg	Town	Central part of Schleswig	Flensburg
Frederiksstadt	Town	South west Schleswig	Friederichstadt
Fredericia	Town	Jutland	Friedericia
Frøslev	Village	North of Flensburg	
Gråsten	Village and castle	Central part of Schleswig	Gravenstein
Gottorp	Castle	Schleswig town	Gottorf
Haderslev	Town	North Schleswig	Hadersleben
Helligbæk	Small stream	North of Isted	Helligbek
Itzehoe	Town	Holstein	Itzehoe
Langesø	Lake	North of the town of Schleswig	Langesee
Lyksborg	Town and castle	East of Flensburg	Glücksburg
Mysunde	Village	Northbank of the Schlei	Missunde
Nybøl	Village	Sundeved peninsula	Nübel
Oversø	Village	Southwest of Flensburg	Oversee
Øvrestolk	Village	North of the town of Schleswig	Ober Stolk
Ragebøl	Village	Sundeved peninsula	Rackebüll

Rendsborg	Town	North Holstein	Rendsburg
Ribe	Town	North Schleswig	Ribe
Silversted	Village	West of the town of Schleswig	Silberstedt
Skovby	Village	West of the town of Schleswig	Schuby
Slesvig	Town and Duchy	Southern part of the peninsula of Jutland	Schleswig
Slien	Fiord	East of the town of Schleswig	Schlei
Sorge	River	South of the town of Schleswig	Sorgen
Sottrup	Village	Sundeved	Satrup
Sundeved	Peninsula	North East of Flensburg	Sundewitt
Sønderborg	Town	Als	Sonderburg
Sønderskov	Wood	South of Oversø	Süderholz
Tønder	Town	West of Flensburg	Tondern
Trenen	Stream	South of Flensburg	Treene
Vejle	Town	Jutland	Veile
Viborg	Town	Jutland	Viburg

Table 6 Casualties during the war

		Denmark			Schleswig Holstein/Germany		
		Dead	Wounded	Wounded POW	POW	Dead	Wounded	Wounded POW	POW

		Dead	Wounded	Wounded POW	POW	Dead	Wounded	Wounded POW	POW
1848									
Bov	9 April	16	78	0	0	34	143	143	780
Eckernförde	21 April	10	19	0	0	20	52	—	58
Sleswig	23 April	170	156	277	249	62	366	0	54
Oversø	24 April	6	4	21	281	3	19	0	0
Nybøl	28 May	34	106	—	11	30	93	40	41
Dybbøl	5 June	59	171	—	17	44	213	—	40
Hopdrup	6 June	11	22	—	22	4	30	—	—
1849									
Adsbøl	3 April	21	—	—	—	8	39	—	11
Avnbøl	4 April	4	23	—	3	3	16	—	—
Ulderup	6 April	56	136	—	18	27	186	—	23
Ekernförde	5 April	106	—	60	898	4	18	—	—
Dybbøl	9 April	18	56	—	4	37	155	—	—
Kolding	23 April	151	374	—	132	52	245	—	109
Borup	3 May	3	24	—	—	—	25	—	3

APPENDIX A: STATISTICAL TABLES 129

Table 6 continued

		Denmark			Schleswig Holstein/Germany			
		Dead	Wounded	Wounded POW	POW	Dead	Wounded	Wounded POW	POW
Viuf	7 May	6	17	—	17	6	40	—	—
Gudsø	7 May	33	111	—	19	7	77	—	17
Århus	31 May	2	6	—	3	2	19	4	19
Fredericia	6 July	512	1344	—	35	202	835	297	1666
1850									
Isted	24–25 July	845	2358	47	368	536	791	411	1090
	12 Sept.	57	159	7	22	14	140	19	123
Friederichstadt	7 Aug.	7	19	0	0	0	5	2	2
	8 Aug.	18	37	9	6	5	14	0	4
Tønning	29 sept.	4	13	14	75	?	?	?	?
Friederichstadt	29 Sept. - 4 Okt.	105	230	2	0	198	481	16	145
Kieler fiord	16 aug.	0	0	0	0	2	3	0	0
Total		2254	5463	437	2180	1298	4003	932	4195

Table 7 The cost of the war 1848–50

Year	The Army expenses	Additional expenses
1848	4,3	8,3
1849	4,5	11,4
1850	4,5	13
1851	—	4
Subtotal	13,3	36,7
Total	50	

The cost of the war 1864

Year	The Army expenses	Additional expenses
1863	18,5	—
1864	18,4	1,1
1865	—	4,5
Subtotal	36,9	5,6
Total	42,5	

The Army expenses are those during a normal year. The additional expenses are incurred due to the war. All cost in million *Rigsbankdaler*.

Appendix B
Orders of Battle

The Schleswig Holstein Army in 1848 at the outbreak of war

Commanding General Prince of Nør

1. Brigade	I Battalion	Major Zeska
Major General Krohn	III Battalion	Lieutenant Colonel Baudissin
	II Chasseur Battalion	Major Michelsen
2. Brigade	II Battalion	Major Kint
Duke Carl of Glücksburg	IV Battalion	Major Bündinger
	V Battalion	Major Schröder
	I Chasseur Battalion	Major Lange
1. Dragoon Regiment		Major Fürsen-Bachman
2. Dragoon Regiment		Major Hansen
Artillery, 2 Batteries	(16 guns)	
	VI Battalion	Being formed in Rendsburg
	VII Battalion	Being formed in Rendsburg

The Danish Army in 1848 at the outbreak of the war

Commander in Chief – Major General Hedemann
Chief of Staff Captain Læssøe
Commanding artillery officer Major de Meza

The Main Danish Army

1 Brigade	1. Battalion
Colonel Büllow	2. Battalion
	11. Battalion
2. Brigade	4. Battalion
Colonel Meyer	7. Battalion
Vanguard	12. Battalion
Lieutenant Colonel Magius	3. Chasseur Battalion
	2. Squadrons
	4 Guns
Cavalry Brigade	3. Dragoon Regiment

APPENDIX B: ORDERS OF BATTLE   133

Major General Wedell-Wedelsborg	6. Dragoon Regiment
Reserve	Battery Bruhn
under Supreme Command	13. Battalion
	5. Dragoon Regiment
	Battery Fuhrman (4 guns)
	Battery Jessen (6 guns)
	Pioneer company

The "Schleswig Flank" Division

Commanding officer Colonel Schleppegrell
Chief of Staff Captain Caroc

- 5. Battalion
- 9. Battalion
- 10. Battalion
- 1. Chasseur Battalion
- 2. Chasseur Battalion
- 1½ Squadrons
- Battery Dinesen (6 Guns)
- Pioneer detachment

The Prussian and Schleswig Holstein army during the advance towards Schleswig 23rd April 1848

Commander in Chief General Wrangel

The Eastern Division	*General Möllendorff*
Vanguard (Prussian)	Fusilier Battalion of Grenadier Regiment Emperor Alexander
	Fusilier Battalion of Grenadier Regiment Emperor Frantz
	Two Companies Guard Sharpshooters
	One Pioneer detachment
	Two Squadrons of 3. Hussar Regiment
	Two Guns
1. Line (Prussian)	1. Battalion of Grenadier Regiment Emperor Franz
	2. Battalion of Grenadier Regiment Emperor Franz
	One battery with 4 guns
	6 guns of the Foot Guard Battery
2. Line (Prussian)	1. Battalion of Grenadier Regiment Emperor Alexander

2. Battalion of Grenadier Regiment Emperor Alexander

2 Companies Guard Sharpshooters

The Western Division
General Bonin

Vanguard
Fusilier Battalion of Prussian 31. Infantry Regiment
Fusilier Battalion of Prussian 20. Infantry Regiment
1 Platoon Schleswig Holstein Pioneers
2 Squadrons of the Schleswig Holstein Dragoons
2 Guns of the horse battery

1. Line
1. Battalion of Prussian 12. Infantry Regiment
1. Battalion of Prussian 20. Infantry Regiment
2. Battalion of Prussian 20. Infantry Regiment
4 Guns and ½ howitzer battery

2. Line
1. Battalion of Prussian 2. (Königs) Infantry Regiment
2. Battalion of Prussian 2. (Königs) Infantry Regiment
2. Prussian Cuirassier Regiment
7 Schleswig Holstein Squadrons

Schleswig Holstein Army
Commanding General Prince of Nör

4 Battalions of the regular troops
3 Chasseur companies
The Braklow Chasseur Battalion (ca. 400 men)
1 Squadron Dragoons
22 Guns

The Confederate Division
General Halkett (this division was not in action on 23rd April, 1848)

Infantry
7 Battalions from Hanover
2 Battalions from Brunswick
3 Battalions from Mecklenburg
4 Battalions from Oldenburg
Cavalry
8 Squadrons from Hanover
2 Squadrons from Mecklenburg
Artillery
28 Guns

APPENDIX B: ORDERS OF BATTLE

The Danish Army April 1849

Commander in Chief General Krogh
Chief of Staff Lieutenant Colonel Læssøe

Als Division

1. Brigade		Colonel Krabbe
	1. Reserve Battalion	
	3. Reserve Battalion	
	3. Reserve Chasseur Battalion	
	2. Reinforcement Battalion	
2. Brigade		Lieutenant Colonel Thestrup
	Royal Guard	
	13. Battalion	
	2. Reserve Battalion	
	1. Reserve Chasseur Battalion	
	1. Reinforcement Battalion	
2. Brigade		Major General Moltke
	8. Battalion	
	9. Battalion	
	11. Battalion	
	5. Reserve Battalion	
	6. Reserve Battalion	
	Battery Marcussen	
	Battery Dinesen	
	Half Battery Tillisch	
	Half Battery Jonquieres	
	1 Pioneer platoon	

Flank Division on the island of Als

Commanding officer Major General Bülow
Chief of Staff Lieutenant Colonel Flensborg

3. Brigade		Major General Schleppegrell
	3. Battalion	
	4. Battalion	
	5. Battalion	
	10. Light Battalion	
	3. Chasseur Battalion	

6. Brigade   Colonel de Meza
    1. Light Battalion
    2. Light Battalion
    2. Chasseur Battalion
    3. Reinforcement Battalion
    1. Reinforcement Chasseur Battalion
    2 Squadrons of Cavalry
    Battery Lumholtz
    Battery Jessen
    Battery Baggesen
    2. Espignol battery
    1 Pioneer platoon

Jutland Division

Commanding Officer Major General Rye

5. Brigade   Major General Rye
    6. Battalion
    7. Battalion
    12. Light Battalion
    1. Chasseur Battalion
    4. Reserve Battalion

1. Cavalry Brigade   Colonel Juel
    3. Dragoon Regiment
    5. Dragoon Regiment

2. Cavalry Brigade   Colonel Flindt
    6. Dragoon Regiment
    Four Squadrons of Cavalry

Battery Schultz
Battery Haxthausen
    One espignol battery
    One pioneer platoon

The Schleswig Holstein Army April 1849

Commanding Officer General Bonin
Chief of Staff Captain Delius

Vanguard	Lieutenant Colonel Zastrow
	IX. Battalion
	X. Battalion
	I. Chasseur Battalion
	II. Chasseur Battalion
	2 Squadrons of Cavalry
	8 Guns
Supply units	Colonel Count Baudissin
1. Brigade	Colonel St. Paul
	I. Battalion
	II. Battalion
	III. Battalion
	IV. Battalion
	III. Chasseur Battalion
	8 guns
2. Brigade	
	V. Battalion
	VI. Battalion
	VII. Battalion
	VIII. Battalion
	IV. Chasseur Battalion
	8 guns
Reserve	
	8 Squadrons of Cavalry
	22 guns

The German Army April 1849

Commanding Officer Lieutenant General Prittwitz
Chief of Staff Major General Hahn

1. Division — Prince Eduard of Sachsen Altenburg
  The Kurhessische Brigade Spangenberg
    6 ¼ Battalions, 4 Squadrons, 9 Guns
  The Bavarian Brigade Schmaltz
    5 Battalions, 6 Squadrons, 16 Guns

2. Division — Major General Wynecken
  The Saxon Brigade Heintz
    7 Battalions, 4 Squadrons, 16 Guns
  The Hanoverian Brigade Ludowig
    6 Battalions, 4 Squadrons, 18 Guns

3. Division (Prussian) — Major General Hirschfeld
  Brigade Kaminsky
    3 Line Battalions, 3 Landwehr Battalions
  Brigade Chamier
    6 Landwehr Battalions, 3 companies of 7. Jäger Battalion
  Cavalry Brigade Ledebur
    8 Squadrons of Cavalry
  Artillery
    22 Guns
    1 Pioneer company
  Reserve Brigade   Duke of Saxe-Coburg-Gotha
    5 Battalions, 2 Squadrons, 12 Guns

Reserve Division — Major General Bauer
  Brigade Duke of Nassau
    5 ¼ Battalions, 2 Squadrons, 6 Guns
  Brigade Rantzau
    7 Battalions, 8 Guns

The Danish Army July 1850

Commanding Officer General Krogh
Chief of Staff Colonel Flensborg

1. Division			Major General Moltke
	3. Brigade		Colonel Schepelern
		6. Battalion	
		7. Battalion	
		8. Battalion	
		4. Reserve Battalion	
		1. Chasseur Battalion	
	4. Brigade		Colonel Thestrup
		9. Battalion	
		11. Battalion	
		5. Reserve Battalion	
		6. Reserve Battalion	
		2. Chasseur Battalion	
	6. Brigade		Colonel Irminger
		Royal Guard	
		1. Light Battalion	
		2. Light Battalion	
		1. Reinforcement Battalion	
		4. Reinforcement Battalion	
		1. Reserve Chasseur Battalion	
		3 Squadrons Guard Hussars	
		Batteries Glahn, Schultz & Budde-Lund	
2. Division			Major General Schleppegrell
	1. Brigade		Colonel Krabbe
		4. Battalion	
		10. Light Battalion	
		1. Reserve Battalion	
		3. Reserve Battalion	
		3. Chasseur Battalion	
	2. Brigade		Colonel Baggesen
		5. Battalion	
		12. Light Battalion	

    13. Battalion

    2. Reserve Battalion

    3. Reserve Chasseur Battalion

 5. Brigade   Colonel Ræder

    3. Battalion

    2. Reinforcement Battalion

    3. Reinforcement Battalion

    5. Reinforcement Battalion

    1. Reinforcement Chasseur Battalion

    2. Reinforcement Chasseur Battalion

    4. Dragoon Regiment

     Battery Dinesen, Baggesen & Just

Reserve Cavalry   Major General Flindt

    3. Dragoon regiment

    5. Dragoon regiment

    6. Dragoon regiment

    Battery Wegener

Reserve artillery   Colonel Fibiger

    Battery Lumholtz

    Battery Marcussen

    Battery Haxthausen

    Battery Mossin

    Half Battery W. Kauffmann & Jonquieres

 Pioneers   Captain Dreyer

The Schleswig Holstein Army July 1850

Commanding Officer Lieutenant General Willisen
Chief of Staff Colonel von der Tann

Vanguard   Colonel Gerhardt

    I. Battalion

    VIII. Battalion

    XV. Battalion

    III. Chasseur Battalion

2 Squadrons of Cavalry
1 battery

Main Army
   1. Brigade   Major General Count Baudissin
      II. Battalion
      III. Battalion
      IV. Battalion
      I. Chasseur Battalion
      1 Squadrons of Cavalry
      1 battery
   2. Brigade   Colonel Abercron
      V. Battalion
      VI. Battalion
      VII. Battalion
      II. Chasseur Battalion
      1 Squadron of Cavalry
      2 Batteries
   3. Brigade   Major General von der Horst
      IX. Battalion
      X. Battalion
      XI. Battalion
      V. Chasseur Battalion
      1 Squadron of Cavalry
      1 battery
   4. Brigade   Colonel Garrelts
      XII. Battalion
      XIII. Battalion
      XIV. Battalion
      IV. Chasseur Battalion
      1 Squadron of Cavalry
      1 battery
   Reserve cavalry   Colonel Fürsen-Bachmann
      6 Squadrons of Cavalry
   Reserve artillery   Major Dalitz
      6 Batteries

Appendix C
Colour Uniform Plate Section

The following colour plates appear with the permission of Mr Jacob Seerup, museum inspector at the Armoury Museum and Naval Museum, part of the Museum of Danish Military History. The illustrations and captions are by Christian Würgler Hansen (captions edited for English readers of this edition by Duncan Rogers).

Plate 1 – Danish Troops I

1. Danish Regular Infantry Lance Corporal

At the war's outbreak, the battalions of the Regulars wore the red uniform Model 1842. The lifetime of the uniform was short; the last time it was used was during the sortie from Fredericia, 6th July 1849. Soldiers from the supply and transport units, and medical units, continued to wear the red uniform throughout the war. The tall black shako was very unpopular with the troops, so the field cap was frequently worn, first the Model 1842 (see figure 3), and then the Model 1848 (see A3).

2. Danish Regular Infantryman

During the course of 1849 the entire army was dressed in the blue uniform Model 1848. Black leather accoutrements were prescribed for this uniform, but the majority of the army was not equipped with them until during 1850. Initially, white leather accoutrements were still used.

3. Danish Light Infantry Battalion/Corps of Chasseurs Private

The Light Infantry Battalions and the Corps of Chasseurs wore similar green uniforms. During 1842 tunics were introduced for the Chasseurs and the Engineers. The field cap is the Model 1842, which was replaced by the Model 1848 (nicknamed the Hungarian) during the War.

A1. 'Swallow's nest' for drummers and buglers of the Regulars. It had the same shape for all branches of service, but the colour corresponded to that of the collars, with zigzag stripes sewn on in the colour of the buttons.

A2. Cockade for the field cap Model 1848. This cockade is the older version, which was abolished in 1842, with a cross in the centre. On all other headdresses there was only a cockade, with one exception, the czapka.

A3. The so-called Hungarian field cap Model 1848. This was light blue for the Regulars and Dragoons, green for the Light Infantry and Chasseurs, and dark blue for the Artillery. The lace along the edge was in the same colour as the buttons.

B. Model 1848 tunic with Model 1848 black accoutrements.

C. NCO distinctions. At the beginning of 1849 the NCO's epaulettes were replaced by metal numbers. The chevrons on the sleeves represent: C1. Lance-corporal, C2. Corporal, C3. Sergeant, C4. NCO. The chevrons were in the same colour as the buttons.

Plate 2 – Danish Troops II

4. Artilleryman

The Artillery wore yellow buttons with crimson collar patches on the Model 1848 uniform, in contrast to the white and bright red for the Infantry. Regimental numbers were worn on the shoulder straps, whereas infantrymen bore Battalion numbers on theirs.

5. Dragoon

During the course of the war, the red Model 1842 uniform originally worn by the Dragoons was replaced by the dark blue Model 1848 tunic, similar to that of the Regulars, but bearing a crimson collar patch.

6. Guard Hussars Captain, full dress

In 1845, shoulder distinctions were introduced for the Guard Hussar officers. On the whole, they were identical with the field distinctions introduced for the whole army in 1849, however by September 1849 the former sleeve distinctions, shown here, were reintroduced. In the field, the Guard Hussars wore either the Dolman (light blue) or pelisse.

D. Czapka, Holstein Regiment of Lancers

The Lancer regiments were disbanded in 1842, however czapkas were used by orderlies during the war. At the outbreak of the war, a volunteer squadron of hussars was established, and due to lack of shakoes, it wore czapkas too.

E. Officers' distinctions

In 1849, in order to make officers less visible, field distinctions replaced epaulettes and belts. E1. Second Lieutenant, E2. Captain, E3. Lieutenant-Colonel, E4. Lieutenant-General.

F. Medical Corps Hospital Flag

Introduced in 1849 or 1850.

Plate 3 – Schleswig-Holstein and German Troops I

7. Infantryman, Coburg-Gotha Infantry Battalion

Amongst others, this Battalion participated in the fighting at Eckernförde, 5th April 1849. As shown here, during the fighting the soldiers wore their greatcoats.

8. Drummer, Prussian Kaiser Franz Grenadier Guards Regiment This Regiment was one of those Prussian units which participated in the War.

9. Fusilier, Füsilier Battalion Lippe

This Battalion was one of the many different smaller German units which participated in the War.

G. Leather helmet for Bavarian Infantry

The helmet is the Model 1848, essentially the same type as that worn by figure 7.

H. Spiked helmet. This was introduced throughout the whole Prussian Army in 1843, at the same time as the tunic.

I. Hussar, Prussian Hussar Regiment No 11

This Regiment participated in the cavalry action at Århus, 31st May 1849. The felt cap was introduced in 1843, but had disappeared by 1850. The shabraque is that for officers. Troopers and NCOs carried black versions bearing a white crown and monogram.

Plate 4 – Schleswig-Holstein and German Troops II

10. Schleswig Holstein Infantryman

During the first part of the War, the Schleswig Holstein troops were dressed in Danish uniforms, or combinations of Danish, Prussian and dyed Danish clothing. However, during the first year of the war, a new uniform based on the Prussian model had been determined and introduced, and is seen here.

11. Schleswig Holstein Dragoon

12. Schleswig Holstein Chasseur

The shako of the Schleswig Holstein chasseurs was not inspired by the Prussians; on the contrary, the shako was not introduced in the Prussian Army until 1854. Until then, the Prussian Jäger wore spiked helmets.

J. Schleswig Holstein Artillery Helmet

The Artillery on the whole, wore the same type of uniform as the infantry, but with yellow buttons and red shoulder straps.

K. 'Swallow's nest' for Bugle-Majors of the Schleswig Holstein Dragoons

L. Schleswig Holstein Dragoon horse cloth

M. Schleswig Holstein Chasseurs field cap

N. Field cap for the Schleswig Holstein supply and transport troops, who wore dark blue tunics with light blue collars, cuffs, trimmings, shoulder straps and white buttons. Trousers were light blue, with black leather trimmings.

APPENDIX C: COLOUR UNIFORM PLATES   145

Plate 1 – Danish Troops I

146 FIRST SCHLESWIG HOLSTEIN WAR

Plate 2 – Danish Troops II

APPENDIX C: COLOUR UNIFORM PLATES 147

Plate 3– Schleswig-Holstein and German Troops I

148 FIRST SCHLESWIG HOLSTEIN WAR

Plate 4 – Schleswig-Holstein and German Troops II

Appendix D

Infantry arms

Figure A1 - Chasseurs firing

Figure A1 shows a chasseur loading his musket (left) and another firing his gun in an upright position (right). The loading process took place by pouring powder from the cartridge into the muzzle. As shown in Figure A1, the soldier could add extra powder from his powder horn. The illustration demonstrates that it was necessary to load the musket in a standing position.

The muzzle-loading smoothbore musket used a round lead ball as projectile which had the same diameter as the muzzle (Figure A2).

The muzzle-loading pillar rifles used a sharp lead projectile which had a slightly smaller diameter than the barrel. For the projectile to grab the rifling, the soldier had to push it down with a ramrod, and push it hard against a little pin (pillar) at the bottom of the barrel. The projectile thereby expanded slightly though sufficiently to grasp the rifling and to prevent the gases from the powder explosion escaping around the projectile. The powder which was poured into the barrel settled around the tap.

The rifle was much more precise and could shoot longer distances than the musket. Both the musket and the rifles were equipped with a percussion lock. This system was invented in 1806 and replaced the old flintlocks for ignition. In the percussion lock, the cock hit a little percussion cap which ignited and sent a spark

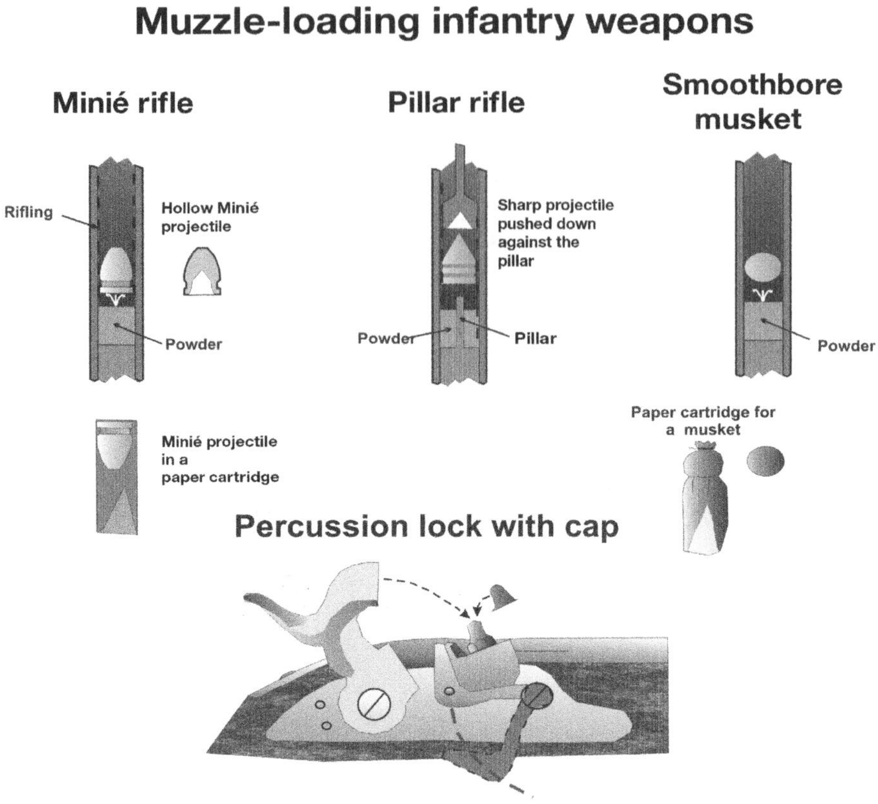

Muzzle-loading infantry weapons

Minié rifle
- Rifling
- Hollow Minié projectile
- Powder
- Minié projectile in a paper cartridge

Pillar rifle
- Sharp projectile pushed down against the pillar
- Powder
- Pillar

Smoothbore musket
- Powder
- Paper cartridge for a musket

Percussion lock with cap

Figure A2 - Muzzle-loading infantry weapons

through a small hole down to the powder which was then ignited. The percussion lock had the advantage over the flintlock that it could be used in both rainy and dry weather.

The soldier could shoot every second minute. In a skirmish line where the men were not densely spaced they could fire in standing, kneeling or lying position. Features in the terrain such as houses, walls, hedges, etc., were often the places where the hardest fighting took place as these were used as cover for the skirmishers.

Figure A1 also illustrates that the soldiers had to fight in pairs in order to support each other; while one was firing the other was loading. This is the reason that the skirmish line is broken into two (figure 2.2).

After the war the Danish Army decided to get the old muskets rifled and use the Minié-system. This system was invented by a French officer in 1847. In the Minié rifle, there was no pillar at the bottom of the muzzle. Instead a sharp projectile was used which was hollow. When the powder was ignited the gas from the explosion was forced into the hollow projectile and expanded so that it grabbed the rifling and became gas tight.

Appendix E

Guns

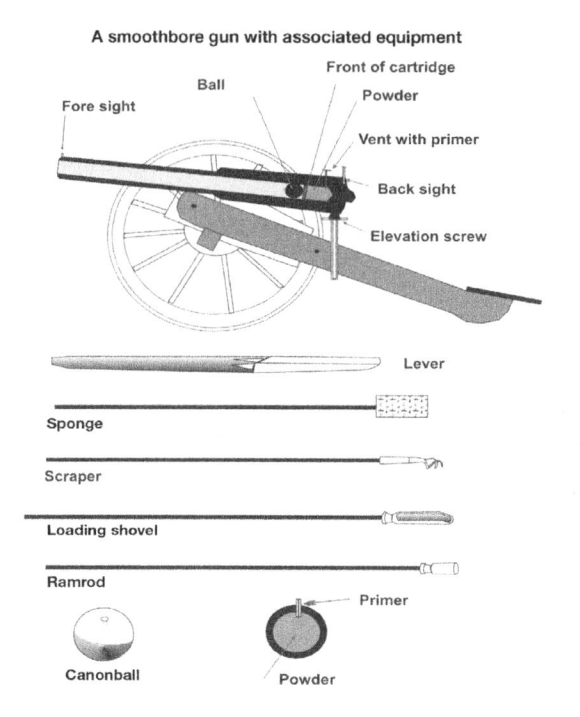

Figure B1 - A smoothbore gun with associated equipment.

Figure B1 shows a muzzle loading gun with the equipment used for handling it. After a shot the gun was cleaned with the rammer, and a scraper to remove the ash from the explosion which the rammer could not clean out. Thereafter the powder cartridge was pushed into the barrel followed by the cannon ball. The cartridge was essentially a paper bag with gunpowder.

The vent in the back of the cannon was cleaned out with a needle and a small hole was made in the cartridge. Finally the primer was pushed into the vent. The primer was a thin tube filled with fine powder and in the upper end with an ignition mechanism which could be activated with a two metre long lanyard. Prior to firing, the gun was aimed using the fore sight and the back sight. The latter was a small vertical metal stick with an engraved range scale. It was often necessary to use the first couple of shots to adjust the aim. It was preferable to hit in front of the target and then with succeeding shots get closer until the target itself was hit. If the shot went behind the target it was difficult to see how far the cannon ball had gone.

In order to handle the gun, the gunners used levers to bring it back to the firing position after the recoil had pushed the gun one or two metres back.

Normally the guns could fire 12 shots per hour. It was not possible to continue shooting for several hours as the guns became hot and needed cooling.

Appendix F

The Cost of the War

The expense of any war can be measured in a variety of ways, but most significantly in the number of casualties in dead and wounded (table 6). During the war the Danish Army had 2,254 dead whereas the German and Schleswig Holstein Army suffered 1,300 dead soldiers. These figures are probably minimal as they only record those slain in the battlefield and dead in the hospitals within the first couple of weeks. O. Vaupel in 1869 claimed that there were 4,000 dead which would make the death rate 32% in the hospitals after two weeks, as the total number of wounded were 5,463.

In order to understand the differences in casualties between the two armies we have to study the tabulations over casualties for all the battles (table 6). If we compare total casualties for the two armies for the battles at Isted and Fredericia only, we can see that the Danish army had double that of the opposing army. These two battles were characterised by fierce fighting with the Danes attacking defensive positions. In such situations you would expect the more protected defenders to suffer fewer casualties. In all the other battles the losses were more equal.

The other way of reviewing the cost of war is the financial aspect as shown in the tabulations (table 7). Denmark reported their total expense as 49.7 million RBD (*Rigsbankdaler*) which is approximately 6.7 billion Danish kroner in today's money. If we compare this figure to the BFI (Brutto Factor Income) which is a measure of the total production of a country - it was in 1850 157 million RBD - the war expenses were ca. 11% of the BFI. In the years before and after the war the military expenses was two to four percent of the BFI. In the 19th Century the Government spent 25 to 40% of its budget on the army.

The war expenses for 1864 are also shown in the tabulations for comparison.

There is no BFI available for Germany but if we use Net National Product we have a measure close to the BFI. The NNP for Germany in 1850 was ca. six billion mark (ca. 12 billion RBD). Germany was split into many small states and there is therefore no estimate of the total military expense. Despite the larger army mustered by Prussia and its allies Germany probably used less than one percent of the county's NNP. Germany had a trade loss due to the Danish naval blockade of the German harbours. The value of this trade loss is difficult to estimate but General Wrangel demanded 2 million species (ca. 4 million RBD) as compensation from the population of Jutland. It is not known if this figure covered the actual loss.

The Schleswig Holstein community received support from Germany, but still used a large part of its resources for the war effort. When Rendsburg was captured the Schleswig Holsteiners also captured the stored Danish military funds there which came to about 2.5 million RBD. This probably only covered part of the Schleswig Holstein expenses for the first year. By comparison the Danish army had expenses for nearly 13 million RBD in 1848. The Schleswig Holstein estate owners complained over the increased taxes as they were funding the bulk of the war effort. Their protest went so far as to propose a peace in April 1850.

The Danish Army probably mustered as large an army as was possible. The Danish population in 1850 was 1.4 million, the Duchy of Schleswig ca. 350,000 of which 100,000 belonged to the Danish speaking population and Holstein had ca. 480,000 inhabitants. The population of Germany in 1850 was 55 million.

Although it seems that the Danish economy was stretched by the war effort, the Danish economy was showing growth and the war effort seems not to have affected the society in the long run. As a matter of fact the cessation of Schleswig Holstein from Denmark had a positive effect. Before 1864 the economic centre of the Kingdom and the Duchies was Holstein. After 1864 the industrialisation in Denmark began to grow but this time in Copenhagen. The agricultural export to UK which previously had been routed through Hamburg was now exported directly from a new port facility constructed at Esbjerg. Therefore Schleswig Holstein may have suffered more by the loss of the trade with Denmark.

Bibliography

Bramsen Bo, *Huset Glücksborg i 150 år,* Copenhagen, Forum, 1975
Brandt, Otto, *Geschichte Sleswig-Holstens, ein Grundriss,* Kiel, Walther G.Mühlau Verlag, 1976
Den danske kommando i Tyskland, *Slaget ved Isted,* Kommando Kurerens Trykkeri, 1950
General staben, *Den dansk-tydske krig i årene 1848–50,* Copenhagen, Schultz, 1867–1882
Hansen, P.W. *Forlade riflen 1825–1865, 1. del*, Copenhagen, udgivet af A. Orloff, Vaabenhistoriske Aarbøger, XXI, 1975
Hansen, P.W. *Forlade riflen 1825–1865, 2. del*, Copenhagen, udgivet af A. Orloff, Vaabenhistoriske Aarbøger, XXII, 1976
Holst, F. og Axel Larsen, *Felttogene i vore første frihedsaar*, Copenhagen, J. Jørgensen og Co, 1888
Hærens Officersskole, *Slesvigske Krig 1848, Infanteriets, Rytteriets og artilleriets organisation og taktiske doktriner*, 1968
Jensen, N.P. *Den Første Slesvigske Krig, 1848–1850,* Copenhagen, Vilhelm Trydes Forlag, 1898
Jensen, N.P. *Oberst Frederik Læssøe, 1811–1850*, Copenhagen, Det Schønbergske Forlag, 1912
Jensen, N.P. *Livserindringer, I, 1830–1867*, Copenhagen, Nielsen og Lydiche, 1916
Johansen, H. C., *Dansk Økonomisk Statistik 1814–1980*, in: *Danmarks historie* Vol 9 ed. H.P. Clausen, S. Ellehøj og S. Mørch, 197*
Johansen, J. *Et hundredeaarsminde om Treaarskrigen*, Copenhagen, Berlingske Forlag, 1948
K., J., *Danmarks kamp for Slesvig i aarene 1848, 49 og 50*, Copenhagen, Universitetsboghandler A.F.Høst, 1852
Korsgård. O. *Interview i Weekendavisen 7 marts, 1996,* Copenhagen, Weekendavisen, 1996
Lauring, *Palle, 1848–1864*, Copenhagen, Gyldendal, 1963
Lindeberg, L. *I lære som landsoldat,* Frederikshavn, Dafolo forlag, 2000
Lüders, Th. *Generallieutenant von Willisen und seine Zeit,* Stuttgart, Verlag des J.B.Messler'schen Buchhandlung, 1851
Madsen, F.S. *Førervirksomhed 1850*, Copenhagen, Hærens Officerskole, 1980
McCue, G. *Brandtaucher – Wilhelm Bauer*, www.Geocities.com/gwmccue/Competition/Brandtaucher.html, 2002
Møller N.Olaf *Tøjhusmuseets bog om Treaarskrigen 1848–49–50,* Copenhagen, Tøjhusmuseet vols 1 & 2, 1948
Nielsen, K.V. *Introduktion til De Slesvigske Krige,* Copenhagen, Hærens Officerskole, 1969
Nielsen, J. *Treårskrigen 1848–1851,* Copenhagen, Tøjhusmuseet, 1993
Nørregård, G. *Før stormen, Christian 8s. Udenrigspolitik,* Copenhagen, Gyldendal, 1974

Rockstroh, K.C. *General de mezas krigs-dagbøger fra aarene 1849–1851,* Copenhagen, Reitzel, 1928
Rosenløv, M. *General Bülows operations plan,* 19??
Tcherning, A. F. *Af Anthon Frederik Tschernings efterladte Papirer,* Copenhagen, vols 1-3, 1876
Thorsteinsson, Hj. *Tiden omkring de slesvigske krige 1848–1850 – med speciel vægt på sanitetstjenesten,* Forsvarets Sundhedstjeneste, 1999
Tuxen, A. *Tscherning, Hedemann, Læssøe, Marts – juli 1848,* Copenhagen, Historisk Tidsskrift, 9 række IV, 1925
Vaupell, *Otto Kampen for Sønderjylland,* Copenhagen, Tre bind. Reitzel, 1869
Vaupell, Otto *Den Danske Hærs Historie til Nutiden og Den Norske Hærs Historie indtil 1814,* Copenhagen, Tre Bind, Gyldendal, 1876
Vaupell, Otto *Kampen for Søndderjylland. Krigene 1848–1850 og 1864,* Copenhagen, Reitzels Forlag, 1888
Vaupell, Otto *Læssoes Levned og aktstykker til krigen 1848–50,* Copenhagen, H.Hagerups Forlag, 1895
Vesterdal, M. *Brudstykker af en fynsk jægers dagbog fra Treårskrigen,* ?, Fynske årbøger, III, 1948
Vesterdal, M. *Slaget ved isted, 25. juli 1850,* Copenhagen, Forlaget Sixtus, 1978
28. ? *Et 125 års minde for udfaldet fra Frederichia,* Frederichia, Frederichia Kommune, 1974
Wikipedia, *Friederich Wilhelm IV von Preußen,* http://de.wikipedia.org/wiki/Friedrich_Wilhelm_IV, 2007